Rhode Island Reds: How To Breed and Judge Them
Chicken Breeds Book 40

by Theo Hewes

with an introduction by Jackson Chambers

Introduction

I am pleased to present yet another title in the "Chicken Breeds" series.

This volume is entitled "Rhode Island Reds: How To Breed and Judge Them" and was authored by Theo Hewes in 1910.

The work is in the Public Domain and is re-printed here in accordance with Federal Laws.

Though this work is a century old it contains much information on poultry that is still pertinent today.

As with all reprinted books of this age that are intended to perfectly reproduce the original edition, considerable pains and effort had to be undertaken to correct fading and sometimes outright damage to existing proofs of this title. At times, this task is quite monumental, requiring an almost total "rebuilding" of some pages from digital proofs of multiple copies. Despite this, imperfections still sometimes exist in the final proof and may detract from the visual appearance of the text.

I hope you enjoy reading this book as much as I enjoyed making it available to readers again.

Jackson Chambers

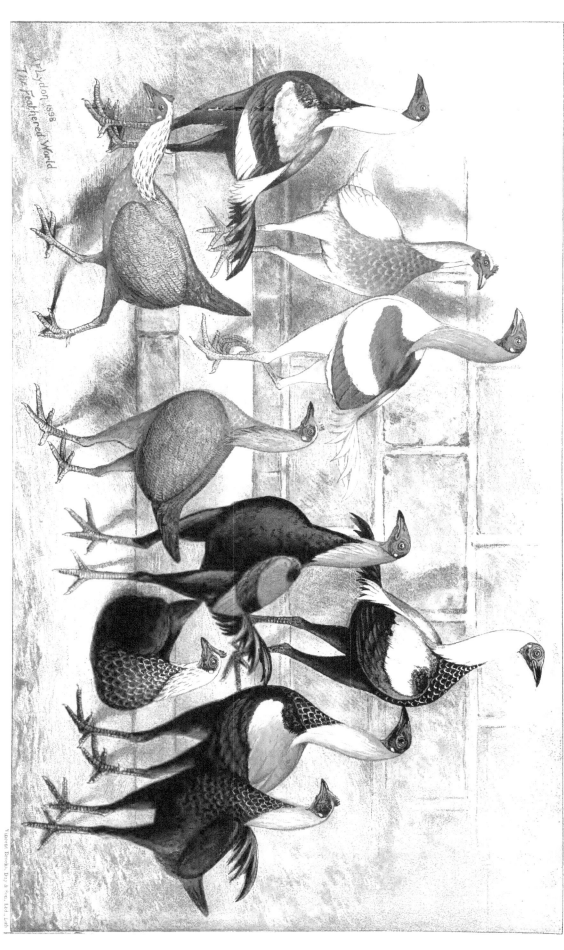

P. Lydon. 1898.
The Feathered World

DUCKWING.   PILE

BLACK-BREASTED RED.   BIRCHEN.   BROWN-BREASTED RED.

GAME BANTAMS.

(Specially drawn to illustrate Mr. Proud's articles on Bantams.)

Vincent Brooks, Day & Son, Ltd., Lith.

A.F. Lydon *Feathered World.*

BLACK ROSECOMB.

JAPANESE.

SILVER AND GOLDEN SEBRIGHTS.

BANTAMS.

BRAHMAS.

WHITE ROSECOMB.

BOOTED.

CASSELL & COMPANY LIMITED LITH LONDON

To the Rhode Island Red Breeders of America this Book is Dedicated

PREFACE

No one breed of poultry now recognized by the American Poultry Association as a thoroughbred has created so many conflicting ideas among breeders and judges as to the proper shape and color as described by the Standard as the Rhode Island Reds. Every shade from Buff to Mahogony has been urged by one or more breeders and judges as the correct color, while in shape, no two seemed to agree on all sections.

With this condition existing, the awards in nearly all shows on this class have been openly criticised perhaps more than all other classes combined. Realizing that under our old system we were getting further apart on what really constituted perfection, and believing a work of this kind would harmonize and bring closer together the opinions of our best informed Rhode Island Red fanciers, I have undertaken the task of illustrating and describing the defects as found in this breed and placing on these defects the valuation that my experience as a judge and breeder has taught me are correct. If this work will bring about a better understanding among fanciers as to what constitutes perfection, and how best to punish defects and at the same time assist the amateur to a better knowledge of this, one of America's best middle weight fowls, I shall feel that the time used in preparing this manuscript has been well invested.

Thanking the loyal fanciers who have so kindly assisted in this work with their articles, covering nearly every phase of Rhode Island Red breeding, I am,

Fraternally yours,

THEO. HEWES

Rhode Island Reds

HOW TO BREED AND JUDGE THEM

BY THEO. HEWES

N their efforts to illustrate and describe color our Standard-makers have gone as far as they can, consistently, with the time and means at their disposal, but they have failed miserably to furnish a text book for the inexperienced breeder that will give him the information he desires or that will, in any way, fit him for a teacher—in fact our Standard in its illustrations and text of all parti-color fowls is amateurish, to say the least, and to men of experience is and should be ridiculed.

A single outline of a male and female, showing only surface color in black and white (and this color distorted in many instances in a manner that would make a thoroughbred hen ashamed of her breed) is the best we have offered to the public as yet, and still, with this shortening of illustrations and text, we have a book of two hundred and ninety pages and cover. It is not a Standard of Perfection and has no right to the title. It is simply a descriptive Standard of fowls that are recognized by the American Poultry Association as thoroughbreds and this same system of recognition would not be accepted by any other Live Stock Association.

A thoroughbred, as this term is applied by other live stock associations, must have thirty-one thirty-seconds of the blood lines it represents and pedigrees to prove them. A full-blood must be absolutely pure—a decided difference from the new breed characteristics as recognized by our constitution and Standard.

But can we improve these conditions and keep within the limit of expense? To make a book as large as the Bible in order to go into all the details in text and illustrations to make it perfectly clear, would bankrupt the American Poultry Association, and when such a book was completed it would have to be sold at a price that would put it beyond the reach of ninety per cent. of our present day breeders. No doubt some of our big specialty clubs could stand this expense for one breed or variety, but to combine all of these breeds and varieties into one Standard with the text and illustrations necessary to make plain to others so all may read and understand it alike, is a task that no Revision Board would attempt unless they had a contract from the Association for a straight twelve months' salary, and that salary would have to be a considerable increase over the paltry five dollars a day they receive.

But We Can Help in Other Ways.

While we appreciate the fact that a work not bearing the sanction or stamp of the American Poultry Association would not be considered binding on any breeder or judge, we can be of service to the amateur by going more into detail with descriptive articles that will make plainer the text of our present Standard and by our chart system of illustration throw more light on the sections that seem to be least understood.

The Rhode Island Reds being one of our newest, as well as one of our most popular varieties, from a fancier's standpoint, we feel that a better understanding of the defects as found in the specimens on exhibition at our leading shows would be of interest and benefit to our readers, and we have gone to considerable expense to point out the defects in color as best we can, and place the proper valuation on them.

In our illustration of the male and female (see figures 1 and 2) we show you what we believe to be the correct shape in the two sexes of well-matured specimens. The feathers grouped around the birds show, as near as black and white can show, the correct colors as described by the Standard, and in discussing the several sections I have made such changes in the Standard description as my judgment tells me will be best for the breed.

It is not my intention, neither do I attempt, to tell anyone how to mate these birds to gain the desired results. The best breeders of Rhode Island Reds in this country are yet at variance as to how to produce the best show specimens of the two sexes, and to our certain knowledge some have discarded what they at one time advocated.

There are, however, some points that my judgment tells me we are right and on those points I am ready to stake my reputation.

First. Except in rare cases the same mating that produces your best males will not produce your best females, and when the percentage of both sexes are of equal quality from one mating, you are more at sea as to how to mate them than if bred from double mating.

Breeders of Reds may scout at this idea all they like, but the fact remains that males entirely too light for exhibition purposes; in fact little more than Buff, have produced many of our best show pullets, and many breeders have used males of this kind to produce a pullet strain. The eyes of our Western breeders were opened to this fact when they went East to buy the Tuttle stock, that was thrown on the market owing to the accidental death of Mr. Tuttle. Here they found the pens mated just as Mr. Tuttle intended to breed them, and the light colored males found in some of them set the Western breeders to thinking.

Second. The breeder that gets scared at some slate in under-color of neck and back, up near the wing butts, in his breeding males will not long produce show birds of either sex.

Another point, and you big breeders (not the amateurs) stick a pin here: Brilliant red does not mean chestnut or brown, and as long as the writer has anything to do with the shaping of opinions in poultry judging, the dark, rusty birds will take their position in the class of "also ran" when in competition with the bright red birds that reflect their luster from every section under certain light reflections.

A Rhode Island Red can be too dark just as well as it can be too light; bright, brilliant red means that color and no other. Anyone can breed a smoke ball but not everyone can breed a red bird that shows correct color and luster that harmonizes in all sections. Set your stakes a long way ahead and then work up to them. That is the kind of Standard-making that helps any breed, and in order that we may all get nearer together on what really constitutes perfection and work in harmony on a general revision of the Standard, I will take a step in advance of our present description and assume that where errors are known to exist, they will be corrected.

Let me call your attention here to some color sections in the Reds you are demanding that are different from any other recognized breed.

Your Standard calls for a black tail, primaries and flights of both sexes, heavily laced with black, with only slight ticking in neck of females; no black in neck of males and no slate in undercolor of either sex.

Do you realize what a task you are setting for nature to perform when you demand positive black in two sections with no undercolor to feed it? There is no other

heart to hold onto some birds good in surface, that have some slate in undercolor, to be used in case of emergency.

While on this subject it is well to take into consideration that the Rhode Island Red Standard as it now reads, did not have the same attention as some other breeds when it was adopted. It was not even considered by the Revision Committee that met in Buffalo in 1903, as the Reds were not admitted at that time, and the Standard we are now working under was hurriedly made up at a regular meeting at Rochester, when none of the Revision Board had the time to give this important work the consideration it deserved. It was afterwards corrected in some minor points, but, taken as a whole, it was a compromise of the Standard submitted by the Rhode Island Red Club and a committee of three, of which the writer was a member.

FIG. 1.

parti-color breed in the Standard so handicapped and it is clearly evident to me that you are asking for more than you will be able to gain unless you add an occasional male or female to your breeding pens with slate in undercolor to feed these two sections when they begin to fade.

It is true that you are producing birds up to Standard requirements now, and, figuring that like begets like, you can continue to do so, but don't be led astray on this theory but remember it is only a few generations back where there was any quantity of black in the neck of both sexes, while slate in undercolor predominated. We have not as yet exhausted this dark blood and it may be possible that this one breed, with red pigments in the blood, will produce sufficient black to keep these two sections up to the .... and we would .... the breed at

The Club has since changed their Standard materially (see Red Hen Tales, 1908 edition).

If I was allowed to suggest a color for Rhode Island, one word would suffice; red. In my opinion black should be eliminated from neck, wing and tail of both sexes and the bird be bred to one color, and in arriving at this conclusion, I have not done so hurriedly, but after handling hundreds of the best surface colored specimens I could find at the leading shows and in the yards of fanciers that are today producing the quality in this breed. Why the Red breeders should go wild over a narrow lacing of black on the wing flights, when this color can not be seen until the wing is spread, is something I have never been able to understand. It seems absurd to me. A solid black tail protruding from the brilliant red coverts of a show pullet is a defect in my eye and I believe every color critic in this country would so consider it. It is true the Red breeders are crazy for this black and insist on having it, and so long as the popular demand is for black in wings and tails, just that long must breeders strive to get it. But in this, as many other matters, time has proven that the popular demand was not the best in the end.

It will be noticed that throughout the shape description of both male and female, the word "medium" is used in describing nearly every section. This word that crept into the first Standard ever published in this country is one of the most difficult to eliminate. It means much or means nothing, and as applied to the Reds means absolutely nothing, because it gives you nothing for comparison.

When we say tail of medium length, we give the uninformed reader as much information as we would to use the same term in describing the size of a building or the length of a street. Medium between what? Is it medium between a Wyandotte and a Leghorn? If so, we should describe it as such, but that is just what we don't want to

breeders who were reading the Standard for the first time, and what we should have done was to provide a scale, under the head of "Technical Terms" that would have illustrated our meaning. For illustration: Short, ———; rather long, ————; long, ——————.

Can some of our readers, who are directly or indirectly interested in Standard-making offer a better suggestion? If so, let us have it and in doing so, please bear in mind that the breed now under consideration is long, measured by the above scale.

The Reds, for their breadth and depth, are the longest fowl recognized by the American Standard of Perfection and every section except head and legs should be described as such. The heads and legs are rather long, as measured by our interpretation of length.

There is no breed now before the American public that has the same length and depth of body on females, size and weight considered, as the Reds and this is as it should be. They are the egg producer par excellence of

FIG. 2.

say because the reader may never have seen a Wyandotte or Leghorn—in fact, a description of a breed should be a complete description within itself and have no reference whatever to any other breed.

With these facts before us, suppose some well informed Red breeder, that is a master of language, get busy and make up a word description that will eliminate these errors and make the Standard say what it means and mean what it says.

At the last general revision, the following system was adopted in describing length—short, rather long, and long. The Revision Committee fully understood the meaning as it was applied to the American breeds. Wyandottes, short; Plymouth Rocks, rather long; Javas, long.

In the Wyandottes and Javas we had the two extremes in length while the Plymouth Rocks were medium between the two, but in order to eliminate "medium," we used the words "rather long."

While this description was plain enough to the men who made the Standard, it was not plain enough to the

the meat breeds; in fact, we have here a combination of Jersey and Holstein in one breed, and when you beat this, you will be looking a long time for a general purpose fowl. When we couple with this a springtly carriage and a brilliant red plumage that harmonizes in all sections, we have one of the handsomest middle weight breeds the fancier ever produced.

In the general description in the American Standard of perfection the Reds are recognized as a new breed, and from a fancy standpoint it is true, but as a commercial fowl in the New England States especially, they are as well known as any Standard fowl, perhaps, with the exception of Barred Plymouth Rocks.

In the general description of the breed, we should go more into detail, and if it is possible to learn more of the correct origin of this fowl, no pains should be spared to bring it about.

On another page we are giving what is supposed to be the correct origin. Whether this is absolutely correct we are unable to say, but we have taken it from the best authority in our possession—"Red Hen Tales," and if not correct, the writer of the article and not the editor is to blame.

I do think, however, that our Rhode Island Red breeders should go more into detail with the variety when first introduced as an exhibition specimen and give to certain breeders the credit for producing the colors that have attracted attention, and a plain statement of these facts should be a part of the breed's description and remember this book will live after us. We should, with the assistance of the Rhode Island Red Club, be able to make a Standard that will last ten years and be a credit to the breed and the fanciers that swear by it.

FIG. 3.

We will now take them up, section by section, beginning with symmetry. We will quote from the Standard in nearly all sections and offer such suggestions as to changes as we believe will be of benefit to the breed.

Symmetry.

Symmetry is one of the most important sections in the scale of points but least understood by the average breeder, and we regret to say by many of the judges. Without a thorough knowledge of this section one is very much at sea in selecting the breeding or exhibition birds, and the judge that has not made a careful study of this section has my sympathy in awarding prizes in a class of good specimens.

Symmetry is the first in the scale of points in all breeds except Games, where it is given as "station" and refers solely to the pose of the specimen. It has a valuation of eight points and these eight points are just as much a part of the hundred points considered as comb, back or wings.

It refers not to one section alone, but every shape section in the scale of points, and a specimen to be perfect in symmetry must be perfect in all shape sections and all sections must be so joined together as to make one harmonious whole. Under the heading of "Glossary of Technical Terms," it is described as follows:

Symmetry. Perfection of proportions; the harmony of all the parts or sections of a fowl, viewed as a whole, with regard to the standard type of the breed it represents.

We believe this printed description should be duplicated in every breed in the Standard where the word symmetry is used in the scale of points, as some breeders seem to consider that nothing is of importance except the description under the head of the breed or variety they are interested in.

A Rhode Island Red male to be perfect in symmetry should be up to or slightly over Standard weight, with all sections fully developed. The comb should be fully developed and of a size to harmonize with a well matured specimen. The neck should be rather long, nicely arched, with hackle feathers well developed and flowing well out on shoulders, filling up at sides, making no apparent break at junction of back. The back should be long, as compared to the weight and size of the specimen; broad

at shoulders, with well developed saddle feathers, showing a slight concave sweep to tail; saddle feathers of sufficient length to carry the outline of back; not quite so wide in rear as at shoulder but nearly so. Tail, rather long, carried at an angle of forty degrees from the horizontal, and with sufficient fullness to carry out the lines of back. Breast; deep, full and carried well forward, not rounded like many of the varieties but nearly on a straight line from junction of neck to lower edge of breast. Body; deep, long and sufficient breadth to harmonize the other sections. Thighs and shanks, rather long, well developed, standing well apart. Toes; straight and well spread.

A male bird filling this description would pass without a discount on symmetry, but any one section described above being off in shape would influence the symmetry in just such proportion as that section is defective. In discounting symmetry the following rule will apply: Comb too large or falling over to one side, ¼ out; neck too long or too short, ½ out; too straight, ½ out; scantily feathered, ½ out. Back narrow, ½ to 1 out; roached, ½ to 1½ out; short ½ to 1 out. Tail carried too high, from ½ to 1; too short or too long, ½ to 1; not well developed, feathers being scant at sides, ½ out. Breast, narrow or shallow,½ to 1 out; not carried far enough forward, ½ to 1 out. Body, narrow or short, ½ to 1 as in degree. Legs long and stilty, ½ to 1 out. Wings, not properly folded against sides, ½ to 1 as in degree.

This same rule can be applied to the female in scoring symmetry as the defects referred to would fall equally as heavy on both sexes.

Weight.

Weight has a valuation of six points, and in score card shows has quite a bit of importance attached to it,—in fact, but few, if any, sections have caused so many rows or unsavory acts on the part of exhibitors.

A discount of two points for each pound underweight or in that proportion for any fraction of a pound, has caused breeders to resort to all sorts of schemes to bring

FIG. 5.

their underweight specimens up to Standard requirements. Some have changed the weights on the entry cards; others will attempt to bribe the weight clerk; others will attach weights under the wings of their birds or cram them with grit or shell just prior to the time they are weighed, and in many instances the weak-kneed officials of associations have so tampered with the scales that they will indicate a weight of from one-fourth to one-half pound more than the specimen actually weighs, in short, there have been so many tricks played on the judges that we believe size should be substituted for weight, and leave the whole matter in the judges' hands to say whether or not a specimen should be punished in awarding prizes.

A well proportioned, growthy, young bird is of more value, even though it may be slightly under weight, than a crowded, over-fat specimen that has been forced for the special purpose of gaining a point in the show.

To say that the American Poultry Association can make laws that will prevent faking is out of the question. We had just as well instruct them to reverse human nature, but under the licensed system we can control our judges and they in turn can enforce our laws, and by leaving the question of weight out of the scale of points

FIG. 6.

and going more into detail, describing shape in all sections, we can prevent underweight, diminutive birds from winning prizes, at the same time protect the type of birds our Standard calls for. This system will in my mind prove its worth to the better-thinking fanciers, then weight can be safely eliminated and size substituted in its place. But until this system is adopted, and the Standard made accordingly, the old rule of deducting two points per pound, or in that proportion, for any deficit, will be the judges' guide.

The overweight rule in the American class affects Reds, but not to any great extent, as but few specimens are shown that exceed the one pound over Standard weight, as referred to in the instructions to judges, but should a pullet, weighing six and one-half pounds, be in competition with one weighing four and one-half pounds, the discount for weight would be the same for both—one point.

The rule for cutting for overweight was adopted in order to keep birds nearer to type, and we believe now, as we did when the rule was adopted, that it is a good one. There is a pound leeway for overweight, so that no careful breeder is injured by it, but we have driven a lot of old duck-shaped Rocks and Wyandottes to the hucksters' pens, where they belong.

The rule referred to under the head of "Instructions to Judges" reads: "The American varieties shall be cut for excess of Standard weight at the same rate per pound, or fraction thereof, as for underweight, provided, however, that one pound of excess shall be allowed."

It is well to note here that this rule applies only to the American class, and I call attention to it because some judges seem not to have understood it.

(The rule for cutting for over weight was eliminated at the revision in 1909.—Ed.)

Conditions.

In the scale of points for the American breeds, condition has a valuation of four points and refers to the health and general condition of the bird on exhibition. It is seldom that a severe cut is made in this section, but more often the cut is made in some other section and the two sections checked to show which is at fault.

In scoring condition, the general health and condition of plumage should be given careful consideration; also shape of legs and comb. When a specimen shows signs

of roup or canker, the out is 1; eyes slightly watering, the out is ¼ to ½; plumage soiled or feathers broken, ½ to 1 as in degree; legs scaly or rough, ½ to 1½; comb or wattles torn, ¼ to ¾.

Head.

The Standard describes the head as of medium size and breadth; beak short, slightly curved; eyes prominent.

The Rhode Island Red Club of America, in their Club Standard, has this description: "Head of medium size and breadth, carried in a horizontal position and slightly forward. Beak, medium length and regularly curved. Eyes, sight perfect and unobstructed by breadth of head or comb."

There is a marked difference in the two descriptions and room for criticism in both. The word medium is used by the Standard and the club means nothing, as we have stated before. The Standard description of eyes is decidedly wrong. Prominent, if it means anything, would indicate that the eyes stood out prominent from the head, like a pigeon's, but they do not. The eye of Reds is prominent in color only and fits in the head like a Rock's or Java's.

In length, the head is rather long; the upper mandible of beak is slightly curved, lower mandible straight. The difference in thickness, where beak joins on to head to its end, makes the upper curve, and in this respect is almost an exact counterpart of the Rock's, in both male and female.

The Club Standard says the head is carried on a horizontal line. Our observation of the best exhibition specimens shows the head, when birds are in repose, to be slightly tipped forward.

Comb.

In our illustrations, Figs. 1 and 2, we show what we believe to be the proper shape in the single comb varieties. In Fig. 3 in this issue is found what we believe the Standard calls for in the Rose Comb variety for the Rhode

FIG. 7.

Island Red male, and in order to give our readers a better understanding of this section it may be well to quote here from the Standard as prepared by the American Poultry Association, also the club Standard prepared by the prominent breeders of this variety as found in "Red Hen Tales," 1909 edition. The Standard describes the comb as follows:

"Single, of medium size, set firmly on the head, straight and upright, having five even and well-defined serrations, those at front and rear smaller than in the middle. In Rose Combs, rose, low, firm on the head, top oval in shape and surface covered with small points, terminating in small spike at rear and conforming to general shape of the head."

In describing shape of female, the Standard quotes "similar to that of male, but much smaller," while the

Club Standard describes male and female separately. They describe comb as "single, medium size, set firmly on the head, perfectly straight and upright with five even and well-defined serrations, those in front and rear smaller than those in center, of considerable breadth where fixed on the head." Their description of Rose Combs is: "Rose, low, firm on the head, top oval in shape and surface covered with small points terminating in a small spike at rear, comb to conform to general curve of the head."

In their description of Rose Comb female, they quote as follows: "Comb rose, low, firm on the head, much smaller than the male, and in proportion to its length, narrower; covered with small points and terminating in a

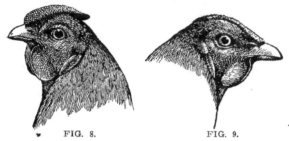

FIG. 8.   FIG. 9.

small short spike to the rear." While it is not our intention to poke fun at the Rhode Island Red Club, we would like to call their attention to their description of the Rose Comb female where it says "terminating in a small short spike to the rear." Do you intend that it shall be the rear part of the comb that terminates, or shall this spike set off at one side or at any angle the old hen sees fit to transmit it? This is only one of several little errors that have crept into the Standard that need time and patience to correct, and it is on these points we wish to spend some time in revision in trying to get as near right as possible, or as near right as our interpretation of the English language will allow.

FIG. 10.

In Figs. 5 and 6 we show two defective combs that while apparently overdrawn, are met with many times in the exhibition room. Fig. 5 would be disqualified for the side sprig at rear, and aside from this is not a bad comb, all things considered, and would be discounted in the show room about one point.

While on this section it is well to call the attention of the breeders to the fact that the comb, more than any other section in a bird, receives the severest cut considering the number of points allowed, as all of the valuation goes to shape and is not sub-divided with color as in nearly every other section in a specimen. A comb that is dis-

counted one is figured as seven-eighths perfect; that discounted two, 75 per cent. perfect, and that discounted four, as 50 per cent. perfect.

In Fig. 6 we have a comb that falls over on one side similar to a Leghorn. While this would not be a disqualification, it would be a serious defect and a defect that is quite common in early hatched pullets that have been laying anywhere from one to two months prior to the exhibition. There is this peculiarity about this defect, that quite often a comb that has lopped as a pullet, afterward when as a hen she has laid out her clutch for the season, sets and raises her brood, the comb straightens up and never shows the defect, or if at all, in only the slightest degree as

FIG. 11.

compared to that when a pullet. However, the comb as illustrated in Fig. 6 would have to be discounted three points and as the score card shows, this would practically debar her from winning a prize, although she might be exceptionally good in other sections.

There are so many types of combs found on our exhibition birds of both varieties that a more detailed description of the several defects, and the effects they may have on the breeding of the specimen will not be out of place.

FIG. 12.

We believe there is room for improvement in both the American Poultry Association and Rhode Island Red Club Standard in general description of this section. The Red breeders from the first have tried to give us a fowl that is different from any other recognized breed, both in shape and color, but in making this Standard they have fallen into the same old rut of all Standard makers and when confronted with a difficult description, have fallen back to the word "description" of other fowls.

We do not believe there are any Red breeders, no matter how many fowls they may have produced in one season, have given certain sections a closer or more careful study in comparison than the writer. The breeder invariably sees these sections from a personal or selfish standpoint, while we have viewed them solely from an exhibition or Standard point of view. The question is, can certain characteristics be produced that will hold year after year and will these characteristics finally mold themselves into a type that can be depended upon to reproduce any goodly numbers without injury to other sections? Every well-wisher of this popular fowl, be he a breeder or revision man, wants the best possible Standard that can be framed and one that will help in making the breed even more popular that it is today, and since comb in all American breeds is of vast importance, I give some facts learned from close study of the best exhibition birds I have found in America's leading shows during the past twelve months. In the Single Comb variety we can not get far away from the Plymouth Rock description, but there is a difference when one studies them from a critic's or artist's standpoint. The Rock head is larger and even in proportion to length, is a trifle wider. The Red is a bird with quicker action than the Rocks. They are more alert and spryer on their feet and when yarded with the other variety a careful

FIG. 13.

study of them convinces you that they cover more ground in one day than a Rock will in two.

In our illustrations, Figure No. 7, we show two combs and two heads, or the outlines of both, one merging into the other, the one with dotted lines illustrates the Rock, the straight lines the Red. Study these carefully and you will find they follow closely the type of the male head of the two breeds referred to, and a careful study of these outlines, we believe, will convince Rhode Island Red breeders that a different description is necessary in order to better enlighten the average breeder. In the Rose Comb, we call particular attention to Figure 8, illustrating the Rose Comb Rhode Island Red female. There is a similarity between this variety and the Wyandottes and to an ordinary observer, they would say the heads are alike, but again there is a difference with a distinction. The Rhode Island Red head is not so wide, although very nearly as long. The comb in this variety is considerably longer than that of the Wyandotte and in our candid opinion, should be a different type, especially so if you desire to make the Rhode Island Reds a distinct breed with new breed characteristics. The rear part of the comb, usually termed the spike, should not follow the base of the skull so closely as the Wyandotte, but should be slightly elevated; not like the Hamburg, on a straight line, but almost half way between the Hamburg and the Wyandotte. Now breeders, please do not get prejudiced to some individual specimen that you own, but look at them as we have and study them as carefully as we have, and I believe you will agree with

us that this type of comb should become Standard and can be reproduced without injury to any other section of your bird and at the same time will give you a head distinctly Rhode Island Red and one that will not be confused with that of the Wyandotte.

In Figure No. 9 we illustrate a defect that is common in Rose Comb Rhode Island Reds and one that I wish to warn the breeder against. It is a long, slender comb, narrow on top, only about twice the width of a single comb and one that almost invariably throws a lot of single comb chicks.

A fault with this style of comb is that it is almost invariably followed by other defects in the same specimen that to us would indicate that it is a defect from a breeding standpoint and should be seriously punished when found in the show room. Our observation of birds with

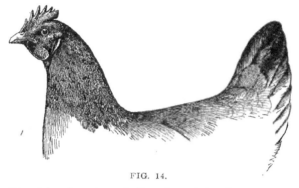

FIG. 14.

this style of comb on both male and female, more especially so on female, shows that it is accompanied by a long, slender, gamy head, with long, scantily-feathered neck, narrow back and sharp pointed tail. A comb like this, though it may be smooth on top, should be discounted two points in the show room and is dangerous in the breeding yard and should be used only when it is possible to mate with it the male with a wide, even surface comb.

While on this section, we again refer our readers to Figure No. 7, and in studying this picture, we will ask that you compare it with the best birds in your own yard and I think you will find that your best Single Comb males have a comb that is higher and broader in front than a Rock, that the comb is more rocker shape, following the skull closer than the Rock. Please understand that in making out conclusions we have studied the photos of more than twenty first prize males of both breeds and we have found

FIG. 15.

that it is the exception, and by no means the rule, when Reds show a comb that conforms to Rock shape. With these facts before us, backed up by the actual photos from birds that have won the leading prizes under our best judges, it is easy to see that all that is necessary to make the Reds distinct in head points is to get a description of them as found in the best specimen to today. Instead of following the old stereotype description that has been repeated since Standard poultry was young, let us describe them as they are and make of them what they are in truth—a distinct breed. It seems to me that it might be well to eliminate the description of both the standards and make an entirely new one, using as our models the best that has been produced, valuing all the defects in them and working the Standard to correct these evils. Then and not until then, will you have a Standard that describes an ideal bird and one that if produced would score an honest one hundred points.

There are a few defects common in the combs of this breed that might well be called up here and a valuation placed on them. In Figure No. 10 is shown a comb that is slightly twisted—too high and long and has three extra serrates. This comb should be discounted three points. In Figure No. 11 is shown a Rose Comb quite often met with. It is decidedly too large, is hollow in the center, uneven on surface and spike turns to the side at rear. This comb should be discounted three points. In Figure No. 12 is shown a comb that conforms closely to the Standard in size and general shape, but has two extra serrates, the last one running back on to the blade. This comb should be discounted 1½ points; one point for the two extra serrates and a ½ point for serrate on blade.

I wish to again call attention to surface color of males. We are coming into a time of year when breeders are making up their yards for the season and they should have this information now. Brown, chestnut or ocher is not red no more than buff is red, and I regret to say that many of our judges are absolutely color blind. Birds are winning east and west that have not a single red section in them. To say that red cannot be produced is all bosh. We have found it on any number of birds without a sign of buff or chestnut, and these birds invariably give us the most brilliant reflectory surface colors to be found in any shade of Rhode Island Reds. Starting with this color in your breeding pens this year, be careful in the selection of females and, my word for it, you will have better colored males and more even colored females from the same amount of

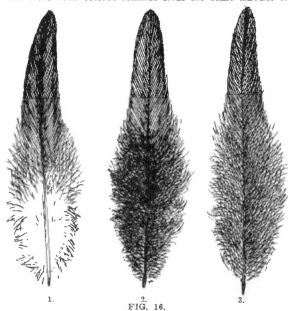

1.   2.   3.
FIG. 16.

birds produced than you have ever had in the past. Keep away from chestnut and do not get scared to death at a little slate in the under color.

The farther we go in the Rhode Island Red Standard in our efforts to score the breed on paper so that all may understand the defects alike, the more thoroughly we convince ourselves that no one text in the present Standard needs revision so badly as this one. The word "medium" seems to have been a by-word for both of the American Poultry Association and the Club Committee that framed the word "description."

In describing the wattles and ear lobes the Standard says wattles of medium size, equal in length, moderately rounded; ear lobes rather small almond shaped, fine in texture. The club Standard says wattles medium and equal in length, moderately rounded; ear lobes fairly well developed, symmetry and proportion in head adjuncts are to be considered. We find that both standards give the wattles and lobes of the female the same description as males. In other words the same wattles that fit the male are good enough for the female. We do not believe any intelligent Red breeder would agree to this when the matter is brought to their attention. We have no desire to call up these errors only as an illustration of just how far we may go wrong in Standard making unless we stop to analyze or prove our work by careful application of the Standard in

Now, let us compare this hastily worded description with one that was framed more than fifteen years ago, describing the same sections on another breed. It shows us HOW MUCH WE HAVE NOT LEARNED in that time. Please study the following description carefully:

Male: Wattles pendent, rather long, well rounded, thin and smooth, fine in texture; ear lobes well defined, hanging about two-thirds as low as wattles, very fine in texture and free from discolorations, which is highly objectionable.

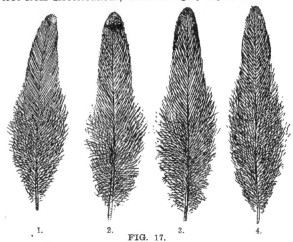

1.   2.   FIG. 17.   3.   4.

Female: Wattles small, nicely rounded, fine texture; ear lobes fairly well defined, fine texture and free from discoloring, which is very objectionable.

This description, old as it is, gives us a good general idea how the wattle and lobes should be, and enables a judge to discount the poor ones, and give preference to those that can be understood by any intelligent reader, whether they be fancier or novice. While the latter description does not fit the Reds in every particular, we have a description on which to build a Standard, and the only change we would suggest in describing wattles would be in the male. We have carefully studied the head points on our best exhibition specimens, and we find in cock birds that ear lobes do not fit smoothly to the heads as many imagine; they are loose on the head, the lower end reaching a trifle below the middle of wattle. The ear lobes of a male are not almond shape, but are rather oblong, being a trifle wider in center than either top or bottom. The wattle of a well developed male is pendent, rather long and well rounded at lower ends, thin, smooth, and fine in texture, while those of a female are small, fitting close to the lower mandible and throat, a trifle broader than long.

It is not our intention to go farther in detail with the minor sections than we believe is necessary to assist the amateur to a full knowledge of what really constitutes perfection, but we do aim to impress on the minds of all

FIG. 18.

breeders the effects some of the minor sections may have on the breeding of the specimen, and experience has taught us that the male or female with well developed combs, wattle and lobes invariably prove our best breeders. In fact, a well matured male bird with small undeveloped or shriveled up wattles, as illustrated in Fig. 13, is worthless as a breeder, and one is wasting the time of a flock of females to mate them to him. In this, as other fine points of breeding, study nature. Your own flock is your school of poultry knowledge. Watch your birds when at liberty;

where a number of males are running with the same flock of females, did you ever find one of those snakey headed, shriveled up wattled birds rule the harem? Did you ever see the hens mate up with them? If you haven't studied this feature then spend a part of your next idle day taking lessons from little Biddy. Her choice of males is the one that can rule the flock by whipping every other male bird in the yard. There is considerable importance attached to the wattles and lobes of the Reds by the breeders and judges, and we will call attention to a few of the defects that are usually discounted.

Wattles: Uneven in length, ½ to 1 out; shriveled or drawn, 1 to 1½ out; when torn or injured by frost or fighting, ½ to 1 out. The Standard calls for a bright red lobe in both sexes and disqualify where the lobes are more than half white. We have been asked by exhibitors if one lobe more than half white would disqualify. Our answer is no, providing one lobe is red; as Standard says "lobes," using the plural, and we presume by this wording that both lobes must be more than half white to disqualify. While the

this variation of opinion among the best informed breeders the Standard makers are more or less at sea as to how to frame a Standard that will be satisfactory to all. Our Standard describes the neck of the male as medium in length, hackle abundant, flowing over the shoulders, not too loosely feathered. They fail to give any color description of neck; still this Standard is good enough for the Red Club or at least they voted it so at New York. The Club describes neck of male, neck of medium length and carried slightly forward; it is "covered with abundant hackle, flowing over shoulders, but not too loosely feathered; in color red harmonizes with back and breast."

In females our Standard describes the shape of neck as of medium length, hackle moderately full; in color red, lower hackle feathers ending with black tips. The club

FIG. 19.

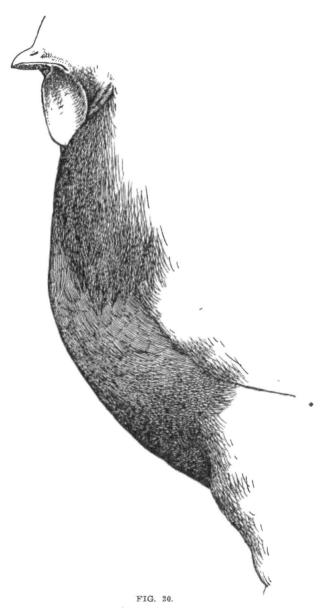

FIG. 20.

shape of the lobes on both male and female are described as rather small, almond shape, fine in texture, we would hardly know how to make the two harmonize in the show room. In fact, a perfect lobe on each sex as nature provides them would have to be discounted on the male or female, and especially so if we were to take the lobe of the male as an ideal for the female, as they fail in the almond shape and are decidedly oblong, a trifle wider in center than at ends, and should be smooth on the surface and free from folds or wrinkles. Where wattles are rough or uneven on surface the out would be ½, where folded or wrinkled ½ out, where specked as we sometimes find them where males have been fighting, the out is from ¼ to ½. In color any sign of white should be discounted ½ point. Where they show one-third or more white the out should be from 1 to 2 as in degree.

Neck: This one section has caused more contention among Red breeders than all the rest of the birds so far as color is concerned. The ticking in neck of the female, admired by some people, is an eye-sore to others. Some insist that it is the most beautiful section in the female, while others claim it detracts from the beauty of the bird. With

describes the neck of females in shape as of medium length and carried slightly forward, hackles sufficient, but not too coarse in feather. In color red. The tips of the lower hackle feathers should have a black ticking, not a heavy lacing. With the above description as a guide, about how near any judge would come to selecting the same bird twice or two judges agree on the same specimen as to perfection, especially so were they to judge the class without consulting one another. When we compare the birds that are considered by the experts as about right in shape we do not vary much from the illustration of Mr. Sewell of the male, as found in the present Standard. On females he is about as far off as an artist could get. While the club's ideal of the single comb female looks like she was hunting for bugs in the next county, the way she has her neck stretched out reminds one of a rubber baby that had been used by some ambitious youngster in cutting his teeth. A hen that would take such a pose in the yard should be sent to the hospital, for she has unmistakable signs of cholera; her legs have gotten stiff under her and she is trying to make her neck pull them along. If her legs were placed side by side, dividing the distance between them as shown in the illustration she would fall over on her head.

The neck of the best shaped males we have handled are rather long, closely feathered around the head and upper neck; lower neck moderately feathered with only sufficient hackle to prevent any break between neck and back.

The neck of the female is long as compared to others of the American breeds, closely feathered on upper neck, moderately feathered on lower neck, with rather scant hackle that flows only slightly on the shoulders. In color the male should be rich, brilliant, reflectory red, free from smut, buff or chestnut tinge in either surface or under color.

The female should be red, free from smut or chestnut in under color. The upper part of hackle red to ends or feather. Lower hackle slightly tipped with black at outer

FIG. 21.

end of feathers. The more one studies the Reds the more convinced they will be that they are a distinct type of fowls. There is no other Standard breed just like them in any one section. While they do possess both Plymouth Rock and Wyandotte characteristics, there is a slight difference when the tracing of one is placed over the other as illustrated in the comb of the male. See Fig. 7. There is a sort of Leghorn carriage in the female when studied on the lawn, as they have that sprightly movement, being quick and alert, but they are not so easily frightened as a Leghorn. Go among a flock of Leghorns and you are the center of attraction; every move you make they have one eye on you while the Red simply tends to her own business, keeps her distance, but moving around as though you were of no more importance than a post or a tree.

One thing we must avoid in the female is to keep them broad and deep enough for their length and always keep in mind the fact that the female and not the male is the one to look to for size in the offspring. The male will give the shape, but the female, in nearly all varieties of live stock, has most to do with the size, and a few careless matings of Reds will give you a type like Fig. 14. Note slim, narrow head, scantily feathered neck, narrow back and high tail. These are a few of the defects one may look for if size in females is neglected; and while discussing the outline, Fig. 14, it will not be out of place to call attention to the several sections and place the valuation on

them. Head too long or too narrow, 1 out; neck too straight and scantily feathered, 1 out; back too narrow, 1½ out; tail too high and pinched, 1½ out. In Fig. 15 we find nearly the same defects in the male. The head is too long and thin, 1 out; wattles too long and narrow, 1 out; neck too straight and scantily feathered, 1½ out; back narrow and slightly roached, 2 out; tail scantily feathered, lacking in coverts so much desired by breeders of this fowl, 2 out. In Fig. 16 is shown a group of feathers that illustrates some of the common defects in the hackle of a male. Feather No. 1 shows white at base and slight dark

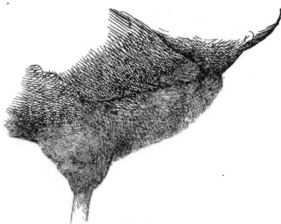

FIG. 22.

lines on shaft at end. A neck showing feathers like this should be discounted 3½ points and never used in the breeding yard. Feather No. 2 is dark at the base, but shows well in outer end. A neck showing feathers like this should be discounted 2 points and should never be used in the breeding yard unless you find color is fading and some black must be added to strengthen it; and even then you are taking dangerous chances unless you know your blood lines on both male and female sides for several generations back. Feather No. 3 was drawn to illustrate a Standard or ideal feather but the artist has the shaft a trifle too strong and shows a slight streak of black at points, and should be discounted 1 point. In Fig. 17 are found four feathers selected from the neck of a female. No. 1 is our

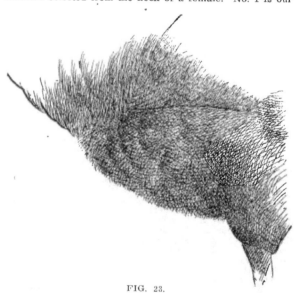

FIG. 23.

ideal of lower hackle feather, red with small black tick or tip at end. We believe this is the color the majority of Red breeders want, and we would not discount it. Feather No. 2 is too black at end, making this section look smutty at junction with back, and should be discounted 1 point. Feather No. 3 has one of the worst defects to be found in the hackle of females. It shows the lacing of black around the lower end of feather like a Golden Wyandotte and should be discounted 2½ points. Feather No. 4 is good in color except it lacks the black ticking at base, and since there is so much stress laid on this section by breeders it should be discounted 1½ points.

Back.

This section in the Reds, like nearly every breed, is one of the most important, both from a breeding and exhibition standpoint. No matter how good some other section may be with a poor shaped or poor colored back the specimen, either male or female, has only ordinary value. The Standard makers realized this and gave it a valuation of twelve points in all American breeds. These twelve points are divided equally between shape and color. The Standard describes shape of back in male as broad, long, carried nearly horizontal with slight concave sweep to tail; saddle feathers of medium length; abundant. In color they overlooked this important section. It might be buff, red or

pullet not yet matured it will look somewhat narrow in proportion to the length of her body. The curve from the horizontal to the hackle or tail should be moderate and gradual. In our illustration of ideal female, we show what we believe to be the correct shape of the back in a well matured female, whether pullet or hen. The club Standard is apparently describing this section to cover all stages from the cradle to the grave, but the judges and breeders should have a description that will describe an ideal back, whether on a hen or pullet, and in mature specimens there is no difference, for when back broadens by age all other sections enlarge in proportion, and a well shaped back on a pullet is a well shaped back on a hen, or vice versa. The cub Standard is in error in describing the concave sweep

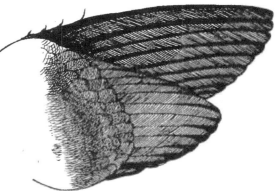

FIG. 25.

at the neck in both sexes, the back is horizontal at this point, it is the hackle feathers that make a concave and they are described in an entirely different section. The back of both sexes of the best specimens we have found are broad, long and horizontal from junction of neck to where tail coverts join this section, where there is a slight concave sweep to main tail. In color the male should be rich, brilliant reflectory red, free from foreign color of any kind, the general surface of back to harmonize with neck, hackle and shoulders. Female: The color should be surface, red, free from shafting or mealy appearance; undercolor red, free from buff, white or slate; shafts of feather red.

FIG. 24.

FIG. 26.

white, and no discounts could be allowed. The club Standard describes it in shape as broad, long, and in the main nearly horizontal; this horizontal effect being modified by slightly rising curve at hackle and lesser tail coverts. Saddle feathers medium length and abundant.

In color the Rhode Island Red Club apparently did not want to offend the American Poultry Association by adding a color description, so they left it out except where they refer to it in a general description of plumage.

In female the Standard describes shape of back as long, carried nearly horizontal, but fail to give us any description of color. The club gives us a description of the shape but, like the Standard, ignores color. They describe shape as follows:

Long in the main, horizontal; in the completely matured hen, it would be described as broad, whereas in the

We wish to again call attention to Fig. 14. Here we find the narrow back with high tail and scantily feathered neck. A back like this should be discounted 1½ points. In Fig. 15 we find the same defect as in 14, except the back is slightly roached in center. A back like this should be discounted 2 points. In Fig. 18 we find a back broad enough to conform to the Standard, but it is deficient in length; in fact more after the type of our Wyandottes and should be discounted 2 points.

Breast.

Here is another important section, it has a valuation of 10 points equally divided between shape and color. The Standard describes the shape of males as deep, full and well rounded. In females, broad, deep, full and well rounded. The word "broad" was omitted from the description of the male, and may possibly be a typographical error, but it does not appear in the Standard. However, if it is desirous to have a broad breast on a female it is undoubtedly just as important that we have it on the male.

The club Standard, in describing the shape of breast of male, describes it as broad, deep and carried in a line nearly perpendicular to the base of the beak, at least it should not be carried anterior. In describing breast of female the club Standard gives the same general description as male, except that the words, "broad, deep" have been transposed and these three words added, "to that line." Neither Standard describes the color, so it will be necessary to make one. In the best specimen we have found the surface color in both sexes is dark red, free from shafting or

FIG. 27.

mealy appearance. This color should harmonize one feather with another so that the same general shade is maintained over the entire section. Undercolor should be red, free from buff, white or slate; quills of feathers red.

In shape the Standard describes the breast of the female as broad, but omits this in describing the breast of the male, while the club Standard calls for it in both sexes. The breast of the male is quite prominent on a good specimen and is carried something after the type of the Rocks. Not quite so high up as the Plymouth Rocks, but nearly so. The Reds are longer for their weight and stand nearer horizontal than any of our American breeds, the head being carried a trifle forward, has a tendency to lower the breast to a point nearly on a parallel with the vent. In Fig. 19 is shown the outline of a breast that conforms to our ideas,

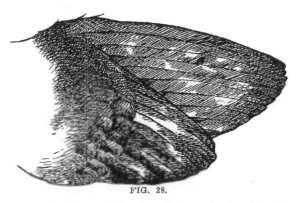

FIG. 28.

and we should pass this without discount, while Fig. 20 is too shallow and narrow, making the specimen look short when viewed from the side and not deep enough when viewed from above. The breast in Fig. 20 is carried too high, more after the type of a young Plymouth Rock cockerel, and should be discounted 1½ points. Where breast is carried forward as it should be, but is not filled in well at sides, the cut is 1.

Body and fluff are included in one section by the Standard, while the club divides the two. The Standard gives the same description for both male and female and we believe this description is good, as it fits the best specimens we have found in this breed; body broad, deep, long, keel bone long, straight, extending well forward, giving body an oblong appearance; feathers carried close to body, fluff moderately full. The club Standard says the keel bone should extend well forward and back. We disagree with them here—the keel bone does not extend any farther back

in the Reds than it does in other American breeds, nor should it. They are one of our heaviest layers and the posterior portion of the female is long, broad and deep. The egg bag is well developed even in pullets before they deposit their first egg. Body in many of our important breeds has not been given the consideration they deserve by breeders or judges, and we wish to emphasize the importance of this section in the Reds. This breed has the egg type par excellent, and nothing should be done by breeders or Standard makers that will have a tendency to injure this section. Appreciating the importance of the body as we do and realizing that an article of this kind may live after the writer, we show here two drawings that illustrate the difference between a really valuable specimen and one worth only her market value. In Fig. 21 is shown the well developed posterior portion of female that was in her best laying condition. This bird layed three eggs in four days while in our charge, and is a type that Red breeders must perpetuate if they keep up the breed's present egg record. Fig. 22 shows the longer legged, shorter bodied type that often win on color over birds far superior to them in shape. It is this type of birds that will ruin the Reds as a commercial fowl and make of them only a show

1.   2. FIG. 29.   3.

bird, and here I wish to caution both breeders and judges on this type of female; when shown as a hen she will invariably show better color than her heavier laying sister, for the simple reason that she has not laid eggs enough to affect her color, while a heavier layer has to use her energy to produce her eggs and as a result her plumage has faded. Observing breeders have noticed this and there was reason in their argument when they advocated a different color description for pullets and hens, and while we are not ready to say that we advocate this system ourselves, we will say that we are making a careful investigation along this line, and if we find that a majority of our best laying pullets cannot be brought to pullet color as hens, then we shall not only favor it but do everything in our power to bring it about. The fanciers that have forethought enough to read the future of a breed are quite often termed a crank, by his less observing neighbor, and in order to make ourselves better understood in the shape of body of Reds, we show two illustrations of males. Fig. 23 conforms to our idea of a well matured Rhode Island Red, while Fig. 24 is the type we warn our readers against. The bird is too short in body, not deep enough through, nor wide enough. A bird showing a body like this should be discounted 1½ points. A body like Fig. 24 usually carries with it the high, narrow, pinched tail, long slim legs and narrow back.

But the crank usually wins out in the end, especially so if his advanced ideas are based on demonstrated facts. Neither the club nor the American Poultry Association Standard describes color in body and fluff only as it refers to it in a general description in color of plumage. Really this Red Standard is a puzzle and one that we fail to understand, and we are certainly in sympathy with the members of the club when they voted to leave it as it is—any old color from a snowball to a brick yard. Body and fluff should be red in both sexes, free from shafting or mealy appearance on surface, and free from buff, white or slate in undercolor. Shaftings of feathers should be red to the skin, the color of surface harmonizing with breast, except the rear of fluff, where we find a lighter shade.

FIG. 30.

Wings.

This section has a valuation of 10 points, subdivided 4 for shape and 6 for color. In shape the Standard describes the male as of good size, well folded and carried horizontal. In females rather large, well folded, shoulders well covered with the breast feathers, flights carried nearly horizontal. In color the Standard describes both sexes alike, primaries, lower web black, upper web red. Secondaries, lower web red, upper web black; wing coverts black, wing bows free from black. The club has the same description, except flight coverts black, wing bows and wing coverts red. There is a vast difference between wing coverts and flight coverts. Wing coverts run entirely across the wing, and in all breeds there are two distinct rows of feathers forming the wing bar. Flight coverts are the short feathers growing on the lower part of the wing bow that cover the upper end of flights. The Standard of 1910 will, unless some changes are made, describe the color in this section as follows: Wing bows brilliant red; primaries, upper web red, lower web black, with narrow edging of red, only sufficient to prevent the black from showing on surface when wings are folded in natural position; primary coverts black; secondaries, lower web red, the red extending around the end of the feathers, the remainder of each feather black, the five feathers next to the body being red on the surface so that the wing folded in natural position shall show red.

This is decidedly the best description that has ever been given this section and describes the wing of our best males and females.

In Fig. 25 we illustrate an ideal wing as described by the Red Club, and this wing we believe is the correct one for the breed, providing we hold to the black laced flights and secondaries. In Fig. 26 is illustrated the wing described by the old Standard. A wing like this when folded would show a black bar across, and we know that no well informed breeder would tolerate such a wing in the breeding pen, as it would invariably throw a lot of smut in undercolor of shoulders or wing bow. In Fig. 27 is shown a wing that is all red, there is no lacing on flights or primaries. This wing is often met with in the show room and

is seriously objected to by many breeders. It should be discounted 2 points. In Fig. 28 is shown a wing that is lacking in black, and in addition has a lot of white in it, showing both in flights and secondaries. This wing should be discounted 4 points—two for absence of black and two for white splotches.

Tail.

This is one section that in our opinion has a wrong description of color in both Standards. They call for a solid black tail and we believe they make a serious mistake in doing so. If we expect a red surface and undercolor on back of both sexes, with no slate, we cannot hope to produce solid black tails for any length of time, and we fail to see the beauty in such. To our mind feather No. 2 in Fig. 29 should be Standard. This feather is red at the base and black at top, and we believe can be bred with a red back and neck. Feather No. 1 is the one our Standard calls for, but there is not one good surface colored bird out of an even hundred that shows a tail like this. As the Standard now reads, feather No. 2 would be discounted 2 points, while feather No. 3 would be discounted 5, or the full amount of the color section. When the Standard for 1910 was submitted at Niagara Falls in 1909, we tried our best to persuade the members of the Rhode Island Red Club to allow red at base of main tail feathers, but they insisted on this description remaining as it was in the old Standard, and it was finally adopted in that way. We are positive this was an error, and we believe that at the next

FIG. 31.

revision, in 1915, these same breeders will ask for the Standard the Revision Committee suggested on tail color, which read as follows: Tail black, shading into red at base.

The club Standard describes the tail of female as black or greenish black, while the American Poultry Association describes it as black, except two top feathers, which may be edged with red. In shape there is only a slight difference in the wording of the two Standards, except the American Poultry Association Standard says it should be carried at an angle of 40 degrees. Both Standards describe the tail of male as of medium length, well spread, with sickle slightly beyond the main tail, lesser coverts rather abundant. In Fig. 30 will be found an outline that we believe conforms to the general description of both Standards, but were we drawing our ideal we would elevate the sickles and have them extend about one inch farther at rear. This would do away with the bunchy appearance that is noticeable in this drawing. In Fig. 31 we find a tail that is carried too high and is slightly deficient in coverts. A tail like this should be discounted 1½ points.

Legs and Toes

are described by both Standards as medium length. In

yellowish horn in front and rear; in males showing of red 32 will be found three defects often met with in all breeds, and Reds are no exception. No. 1 is knockkneed and should be discounted 1½ points. No. 2 shows scaly legs, illustrating how the insects are working under the scales, making the leg look swollen or out of proportion, and should be discounted ¾ point. No. 3 has two crooked toes and should be discounted 1½ points.

We feel that a careful study of the defects as referred

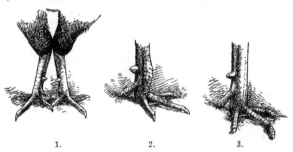

1.   2.   3.

FIG. 32.

fact, the word "medium" is used in every section where the Standard makers were at a loss to find a word to fit the case. A better description would be rather long, as both sexes are usually well up on legs. In the male the thighs are large and meaty for the size of the specimen, and feathers on this section are rather long. In the female the thighs are rather long and large for the size of the specimen, shanks rather long, bones stout, smooth and even on the surface, free from feathers or down. In color a

pigments at the side. The female, yellowish horn. In Fig. to in this series of articles, will enable the breeders to select their best specimens, and be able to avoid many of the errors in mating that have caused some to give up the Reds as a fancier's fowl. If we accomplish this we will feel well repaid for our efforts in bringing this meritorious breed more prominently before the poultrymen of this country, as well as foreign countries, where the Inland enjoys a good circulation.

CAN WE HOLD THE COLOR OF FEMALES DURING MOLT?

BY THE EDITOR.

This question is one that concerns every breeder of Rhode Island Reds and has been discussed perhaps as much as any other one subject. Pullets that have the most brilliant lustre early in Spring will show signs of fading as soon as the heavy egg yield starts, and this fading will continue during the entire laying period, and it is rare indeed when any of them nearly approach their pullet color when they pass through their molt and come as hens.

Deny this as we may, cold facts, backed up by the experience of hundreds; yes, thousands bear me out in the statement that no one breed of parti-colored birds is so badly handicapped in this particular as Rhode Island Red females. Some other parti-colored birds are affected, but none in proportion to the Reds, while others are even better as hens than as pullets. This is especially true of breeds with Partridge or Indian Game color. The fading propensities of the Red female are so strong that quite a few fanciers advocated two Standard color descriptions for Red females; one for females under one year old, the other for them more than a year old.

The claim is often made, and we believe justly so, that under our present Standard there is a constant incentive to show well matured pullets as hens, and where the judge is not strictly up to his work this trick ofttimes wins on color alone.

The question is, "Can this color defect in females be eliminated without injury to the egg production, and if so, how?" This is a question that few of you have considered as you should, and it is up to some one of you to do some tall experimenting if you wish to accomplish this. When hens have been confined for a long time or allowed to sit for months, giving the reproducing organs a long rest, we have known where hens come back in the adult with plumage nearly as good as pullets, but we do not want a heavy laying breed like the Reds to be handicapped in this way. They are the egg machines par excellence, and to do anything to injure their egg yield would be doing just that much to injure the popularity of the fowl.

Some breeders are holding color of females better than others. Just how they do this, we are unable to say,

but we know of some strains that come back nearly as good as hens as they were as pullets, while others simply fade out until they are hardly fit to be classed as "thoroughbreds."

We are going to offer a suggestion that we believe will help. We do not claim that it will entirely remove the trouble, and we know it will not replace the black in tails that goes with the first molt of a pullet, but we do believe, if our suggestions are carried out, that most of the lustre found on the surface of our best colored pullets can be reproduced in the hen. This is the plan we would recommend:

During the latter part of July, or the first of August, when your pullets become broody, allow them to sit for four or five weeks. Give them a few china eggs in order to hold them to their nests. This long period of incubation will reduce their weight and deaden their plumage, so there is no life or lustre in it. Then remove them from the nests and give them a thorough washing, using water as hot as the fowl will stand, to which should be added a small amount of kerosene emulsion. (This emulsion can be made by adding soap to a pan of boiling water until the substance becomes thick like syrup, then add the kerosene, about a tablespoonful to a quart of liquid and mix well). Use this instead of soap while washing the fowls, as it will remove the dirt better than soap and at the same time kill any lice or mites that may be on the fowls. Place these hens in a thoroughly clean place, where there is no possibility of lice or mites getting on them and feed heavy of the richest food you can find, such as beef scrap, oil cake, cooked meats, and if you are near a slaughter house, get fresh blood and mix with bran or ground oats. To your soft feed, add a liberal allowance of red pepper. See that the fowls have plenty of charcoal and grit, and we believe that in ten weeks you will have a hen through her molt with plumage nearly as good as she was as a pullet.

While we realize that this requires considerable work on the part of the breeders, it is certainly worth the effort, as to win on a hen in close competition is, to our way of thinking, a great deal more credit to the breeder than to win on pullet, as it shows you are not only a breeder but a fancier as well.

RHODE ISLAND REDS

Forty Years Ago and Today—Correct Color Properly Understood Can Be Bred From One Mating—Let Your Color Be Red, Not Brown or Mahogany.

By LESTER TOMPKINS, Concord, Mass.

In about 1869 or 1870, I had my first flock of hens. I built my houses of two large dry-goods boxes with the addition of some flooring of an old whale boat. My flock consisted of three pullets raised by a red hen that stole her nest and was given me by father if I would catch her. She run in the oat field and was very wild. I secured her and grandmother gave me a pullet and my uncle gave me a pair, a pullet and a cockerel, that came home about that time on one of the whale ships that my uncle was agent for. This was my start in the poultry business on my own account.

These hens were red with black tails, and nice ticked hackles shaped like the Rhode Island Reds of the Standard type of today and were regular hustlers. The males were a bright brilliant red, very rich with black tails in the main. Occasionally one would have nearly a red tail, but those were exceptions. The males also had clear hackles and clean surface color. I never looked at the undercolor in those days, but as I remember dressing them for market, they nearly always were salmon or buff all through. Not all dark and rich as the undercolor of some of our best today, but bright and clear.

We renewed our stock in those days by changing some with another neighbor and also the incoming whale ships occasionally brought in a few males and they were a great help for producing vigor in our flocks. A very few took much pains as to mating and breeding. We, at home, always made a few small matings to get good breeding stock and many came to our place for their breeders each spring and winter. They were a well established breed and run very true to color, but many farmers were tempted to try new breeds as they came along and make crosses with Leghorns, Brahmas and all varieties that were introduced into the country. If they did not like the results they would go back to the old Red stock, but some of this crossed blood showed for a long time and that is where a great deal of smut came from in the first place. However, those who kept the old-fashioned stock continued to produce good birds with the changes they made among the neighbors if they could find anyone who had not been experimenting with new blood, and the best of these flocks were producers of our best flocks of today.

When the demand came from different parts of the country for the Reds and as they became more popular, many birds were sold as Reds that were as much something else as Reds, and also Rose and Single Combs sold from the same flock. No matter which you bought, you would get both.

Most of the farmers who had good blood did not care to sell the stock at the prices then prevailing. In fact, the good, straight, old-fashioned Red flocks were very few and owned by people who knew them well, but it was almost impossible to get a bird from them at the prices then prevailing.

When the promoters of the R. I. Red Club of America, Dr. Aldrich and others from Fall River went to Little Compton, Triverton and Westport and picked up the best they could find there and started breeding them for show and brought them out at New York in the 1892 show, they little thought they were promoting what was to become the most popular breed of poultry on earth.

I was talking to Dr. Aldrich the week before he died, and was looking at his birds, and he remarked: "Tomp-

kins, who would ever think that the little old ren hen would have become so popular and create such enthusiasm in the poultry world?" Their popularity is still increasing to the extent that it is almost impossible to supply the demand and is bound to continue if bred as of old, by single mating, which can be done as it always has been, except the fanciers go crazy over the dark birds. Some are favoring the dull brown color without the luster. That will never do to continue breeding good Reds. It means resorting to double mating, which surely ruins any breed. It is easy to breed dark birds if you want them, far easier than to breed a good, medium, rich red that is bright and full of luster that will reproduce both cockerels and pullets of uniform color from the same matings. I admit I am breeding dark birds, as the trade demands them, but I use them with caution. Take the pen I won with at New York two years ago, which was a pen just as they were shown, that would and did reproduce themselves and still continue to do so as did their ancestors. Yet they were far from a dark pen as they show today.

The pen I showed at New York in 1910 I consider is the extreme of red without going on to the brown and they are very nearly the same color today (May 1st), as when shown January 1st, that after heavy laying all winter. Some of them were laying during the show at New York, January 1st. This pen is a bright red, and I am waiting to see the result after moulting. They certainly have gone beyond my expectations. If we could hold that color in the hens, it is certainly the color we want, but I have no doubt as to the male, as his ancestors for many generations, have been the same. He is a direct descendant from the first and second cockerel at Boston, 1903.

I think Mr. Hewes will remember the first and second cockerels and the first and second pullets at Rochester in 1904, when the Reds were admitted to the Standard. They were bred that season from the second cockerel at Boston, 1903, and the first New York cockerel is a direct descendant from the same lines.

I have the sisters to these same pullets that were at Rochester that I am breeding from this year in spite of what the fashion may be. I shall continue breeding the same as I always have and may hit the fashion once in a while as I did at Chicago and New York during the past season.

Now, as to the style of matings for breeding Reds. They can be bred and are bred in many flocks as I can show, as uniform as any breed. I am asked why many birds from our best matings vary so much. I will answer that in this way: It comes from resorting to extremes in color to produce strong Standard markings for scoring at the shows where competition is strong. Being a parti-colored breed, we sometimes go too strongly, but, as I said before, they can and are being bred on farms as even and as uniform as any breed of fowl on earth.

The greatest trouble in showing such dark birds as some favor, compels resorting to all kinds of extremes to produce the females to match the males. If we could get together on a bright, brilliant red, which we can produce by single mating males and females from the same pens, it would create satisfaction and settle disputes that always arise among so many beginners with the Reds. Of course we expect to vary a few shades, but keep away from the dull brown birds. Let's have them so red that they cannot be connected with any color but RED. After resorting to extremes to produce the show birds to score high we use some of the medium specimens resulting from these matings, for breeders, but just remember that they were produced from extremes. How do you know which way they will produce? They are sure to take one side or the other. As a breeder, give me a bird produced from a uniform

FIRST PRIZE PEN S.C. R. REDS AT MADISON SQUARE GARDEN N.Y. DEC., 1917.
LESTER TOMPKINS CONCORD MASS., Owner and Breeder

mating, even though he may not score so high as some produced from a freak mating, I think he can better be depended on for good results and is more valuable as a breeder.

The Reds certainly have a great future before them and are bound to hold their own as their utility qualities cannot be equaled, also in the show rooms they are certainly most beautiful to look upon.

Out crossing is the way the breed was brought to its highest type of perfection. Now, do not do too much inbreeding.

About ten years ago, when good strains were becoming so scarce and I found many strains so unreliable, I started breeding different lines so as to outcross without going outside of my own flock. To this, to a great extent, I lay the cause of my reproducing so many winners and keeping up vigor and ruggedness, which are the most desirous to continue in the Reds, as that has been one of the strongest points in their favor.

THE ORIGIN OF ROSE COMB RHODE ISLAND REDS

BY H. G. DENNIS, in Red Hen Tales.

Having seen a number of articles in agricultural and poultry journals on the origin of the Rhode Island Reds, and being positive in my belief that I know where the progenitors of the Rose Comb variety came from, with your permission will say:

That forty-five years ago to my knowledge, there could be found on the incoming whaleships, and in the yards of the sailor boarding houses, and those of the Por-

meeting the requirements of the Rhode Island Red standard than the best Reds today do.

In plumage they would excel the present day Reds. They were of an even colored rich dark red of a shade difficult to describe. Both male and female were dark. The males had an elegant glossy plumage, and with what was called in those days a bottle green tail. The females were more subdued in color and had a black tail. They

RED MILL The Third. A Winner At
Madison Square Garden, New York,
Boston, Mass., Washington, D. C.
Richmond Hill, N. Y., Paterson, N. J.
The Alaska Yukon Pacific Exposition.
KAUFMANN & WINDHEIM,
Mutley, N. J. 1910.

tuguese and other foreign residents of that part of New Bedford, bordering on the water front and known as Fayal, as well as on a number of farms within a radius of ten miles of the city, many specimens of red rose comb fowls that were brought from Java, and the adjacent islands, by the whaleships, and called by the sailors Red Javas. The Red Javas would come as near, or nearer, to

had combs of a fine slant, of medium width terminating with a spike, comb full and with prominent serrations, legs of reddish yellow and medium length.

In conformation they were very long on the keel, and straight on the back. They were very active and great foragers and layers. In color there were three varieties of the Javas; red, white and black, all of the same conformation and characteristics.

That the Javas were a true or distinct breed is my belief, as many bantams, miniature productions of the large variety, were to be found in the places that I have before named.

In company with some schoolmates, we had at one time about twenty-five specimens of the Red Javas, about two-thirds of them males. They were obtained in part from the ships, others were bought from the foreign residents along the water front. We kept them in a barn in the center of the city. They soon caused a protest from the neighbors, and we had to dispose of most of the males. They were sold to farmers who brought produce to the city from Little Compton, Adamsville, Westport, Dartmouth, and to the farmers of the towns to the north and east of New Bedford.

As many of the officers of the ships came from the towns above named and westerly along the coast to New London, and vessels sailed from Westport Point and New London, it is fair to presume that some of the Javas found their way to those sections through that channel.

I have kept the Reds many years and would not keep any other breed. That the Red Javas were the progenitors as a whole, or in part, of the Rose Comb Reds of today is my belief, and there is no theory than can be advanced or argument brought forth, that would have any effect on

I am not one of those who is willing to say, "Never mind the origin of the 'Reds' or any other worthy variety of fowls." I have been breeding poultry for twenty odd years, and I am always interested in the origin of every breed. Go back into history with me fifty years, and we find that, at that time, 1846-1850, different Asiatic breeds were introduced into this country, especially in neighborhoods that were near the coast. One variety, the Shanghai fowl (yellow and white), was introduced just after the Cochin China, and the two breeds for a time became confused and "many farmers and poulterers declare, spite of feathers, or no feathers (on the legs), that their fowls are Cochin Chinas or Shanghais, just as they please." At this time, Bennett, in his poultry book, says: "There are but few, if any, bona fide Shanghai fowls now for sale." These Shanghai fowls (Simon pure) were heavily feathered on the legs. Not so with Cochin China. At this time the Cochin Chinas were bred extensively in Southeastern Massachusetts and Rhode Island. Dr. Alfred Bayless, of Taunton, Mass., imported in July, 1846, specimens of the yellow Cochin Chinas. "The cockerels were generally red." These were not specimens of what were called the Royal Cochin Chinas, as bred by the Queen of England, but direct importations, "The Royal Cochin Chinas were one-third larger." The Shanghais were heavily feathered in the legs; these imported Cochin Chinas lightly feathered, if

at all. The ship Huntress, in May, 1847, direct from Cochin China, brought a pair of this variety of fowls, and Mr. Taylor, in speaking of them, says: "The imported cock was a peculiar red and yellowish Dominique, and the hen a bay or reddish brown;" that the young stock varied "only in shade of color," Bennett says: "The legs of both sexes are of reddish yellow, sometimes, especially in the cocks, decidedly red—more so than in any other variety." How many times I have called attention to the red pigment in a Rhode Island Red cock's legs.

So much, then, for the Red Cochin China cock of fifty years ago. The sea captains brought home just such specimens to Little Compton, R. I., but a little later came the great Malay fowl, with its knotty knob of a comb—a comb that even today occasionally is to be seen on the Rhode Island Reds. The Jersey Blues—Bucks County and Boobies—were inferior varieties of Malay. The Great Malays came from the peninsula of that name at the southern point of the continent of Asia. They were spoken of as "serpent headed." Their color was dark brown or reddish, streaked with yellow; some varieties of Malays ran more red than others. In Little Compton, was introduced what was spoken of as the Red Malay. The Red Cochin China cocks and the Red Malay cocks were selected, and crossed with the flocks of fowls in Little Compton, forty and fifty years ago, the same as today. Later, before the Wyandotte fever, the R. C. Brown Leghorn was introduced into many flocks in this neighborhood. Even at the time of the introduction of the Leghorn blood, the Red fowls were spoken of as Rhode Island Reds. In a certain section, a section where the Leghorn blood was not used, today old settlers speak of their fowls as Red Malays; in this section ten years ago, the Reds were all of the single comb variety, whereas, ten or twelve miles further south were to be found rose combs in abundance.

Now, Mr. Editor, let me say right here, and I wish to say it plainly, there practically were no Pea Comb Reds ten years ago, any more than today. Why should Rhode Island Red fowls have pea combs? Where is the comb to come from? It is not the common comb of barnyard fowl. It is not the comb of any of the varieties that made the Rhode Island Reds. I should just as much expect to see the Reds with topknots as with pea combs, and if Mr. Anybody wants to put topknots on them, go ahead, only he can't sail in the Rhode Island Red boat this year. Of course, he can sail in his own boat—and who cares. The Pea Comb Rocks were once admitted to the Standard, only to be dropped again. I do not believe the Red Club will admit Pea Combs only to drop them again. Those that raise Reds feel differently about Pea Combs from some of those that raise their pen and ink simply to write about them.

ORIGIN OF ROSE COMB REDS

Time Required To Establish a Strain—Four More Years Will See Them in the Lead.

By KAUFMAN & WINDHEIM.

For the past fifteen years we have carefully bred and studied Rose Comb Rhode Island Reds. During this time we have come in contact with nearly every known breeder and have talked the matter of their origin over and over again, thrashing the information out and sifting it down until we have finally decided that the Red Javas of fifty years ago were the real ancestors of the Rose Comb Rhode Island Reds of today. Many breeders and writers lay claim to the Cochin China Red Malay cross, which

praise to the grand old Red Javas, imported into New England some fifty years ago.

Being two of the pioneer fanciers in breeding R. C. Reds for exhibition purposes and having established after great effort a strain that is known the world over for its dark color, we are glad to give our fellow fanciers a brief bit of our experience of the way we accomplished the task of obtaining the very dark, but still rich, color for which our birds are noted.

FIRST PRIZE R·C·R·I·RED COCK AT MADISON SQUARE GARDEN N·Y· 1909-10

"YANCATAW"

KAUFMANN AND WINDHEIM NUTLEY NEW JERSEY

has considerable bearing upon this subject, as the Reds of today resemble Malays to a certain extent, also to some degree the Cochin China. This resemblance is most noticeable in the poorer bred flocks, where many may be seen with stubby combs and feathered legs. One of the oldest (now retired) breeders of R. C. R. I. Reds remembers the Javas some fifty years ago and says that at that time they were equal, if not better, in deep red surface color than the R. I. Reds of the present day. From this gentleman's knowledge and our long experience in breeding and studying this now famous breed, we cannot help but sing

Over fifteen years ago, we traveled through New England, sparing neither money nor time, buying the best that could be purchased of this variety, in each case only purchasing the darkest red birds. The following year we again visited every breeder of note in the East and on this trip laid the foundation of our strain. In a country hamlet of Massachusetts, we found a breeder who was noted for the breeding of this variety for a number of years and for having the best flock in New England. This meant "the world," as there were none to amount to anything outside of this section. We purchased his entire flock of 121 head, at a fabulous price for that time for such a comparatively new variety. About four-fifths of these birds were very dark in color; in fact, too dark. With these birds we mated the best of what we had, crossed and crossed, in-bred, out-bred and line-bred, introducing new blood on three occasions, paying large prices for the best, and year after year, could see the ear marks of the Red Javas crop out again and again. In the producing of this dark color we saw as many defects and dangers as with breeding the medium colored birds, for with the medium colored birds many may come buff and mottled, yet the darker birds produced many that were too strong in black, throwing many that were peppered with black all over their body and with too heavy ticking on hackles, also many were of the dark chocolate shade, which is the wrong kind of red. But we kept picking the richest and cleanest of the darkest, never breeding from a bird that was peppered in wing bows or other sections, and have finally brought them to the point where they will breed deep red and the majority true.

A curious thing about breeding for dark color is that very dark males mated to females of medium color produce hardly anything, while very dark females, mated to males of medium color, produce well, but naturally dark males and females produce the best. That all breeders are improving the color of their flocks may be seen by the improvement in the color of the birds shown at Madison Square Garden each year, and we predict that with about two more years of breeding on the color question counting in proper black markings, also laying great stress on undercolor and then about two more years of careful breeding for shape, we shall have the R. C. R. I. Reds nearly as true a breeding variety as the Plymouth Rock and the finest appearing as well as the best all-around fowl that can be bred.

That the fanciers of America, and Europe as well, are expecting this, is noticeable by the great many that are breeding them. It is safe to say that over two million dollars changes hands in this country every year over this breed, counting in exhibition and market values. While the Rocks are a grand old breed, yet mark our words, the Rhode Island Reds will be the fowl. From the conservative old New Englander came the foundation of this breed, into the hands of the fancier, breeder and exhibitor, and now to every back yard in the country, it is an American breed for the American people, that makes the American dollar.

Rhode Island Reds in Tennessee—Look Well to the Size of Your Females—Experiments Must Tell Us What To Do With Slate in Under Color.

The most beautiful is not always the most useful. Beauty has its place in the world and a most important one, as the highest pleasure the brain can experience comes through the avenue of the eye. It is to gratify this love for the beautiful that we breed for fancy plumage, and in serving to please the eye, it occupies a very important place. An indescribable sensation of pleasure is experienced when we gaze with an educated eye upon the even, rich, red plumage, fringed with a tail border of black. Take away the love for the beautiful and the fancier goes with it.

But in our zeal and enthusiasm for improvement in plumage, we must not lose sight of that most important point of size. Persistent line breeding will no doubt bring the color to a very high state of perfection, but care must be exercised in mating so that the birds are kept up to Standard size and proportion. It is a great temptation to feature in our pens small females that are exceedingly rich in color, but we must use care else in a short time we will have beautiful Reds with Leghorn size. The Red hen that has done constant duty for a season and lost her bloom of youth and has taken on a lighter hue may not be so pleasing to look upon, but she is more apt to lay eggs that hatch stronger chicks than her pullet daughter arrayed in her brilliant red robe.

We are awakening in Tennessee to the necessity of maintaining the size of our birds. For many years the poultry industry did not receive the careful attention in this section that it did elsewhere. Now we find hundreds of Reds where a few years ago they were almost unknown. They are fast forging to the front in the South, and in a very few years more I predict that our brother fanciers of the East and North will be finding their most formidable rivals from the land of Dixie.

We can hatch in January and February and have very little trouble in taking care of these early birds. At present there are but few large plants in the South where men give their undivided attention to breeding fancy poultry. Most of our fanciers are engaged in poultry culture because it pleases them. It is their recreation, their divertment. Their wives do the work and they do the blowing. The various household duties of the wives prevent them from bringing their poultry plants to that degree of perfection that could be reached, were undivided attention given to it.

The disadvantage that this occasions is frequently felt in the show rooms, where our brother breeders of

"RED FEATHER II."

First cockerel at Nashville State Fair, 1909. Silver cup and A. P. A. medal for best cockerel in show; A. P. A. diploma for best male under one year old. Bred and owned by James M. Frank, Nashville, Tenn.

the North and West, who are engaged primarily in the rearing of poultry, bring in their birds that have been forced to maturity and groomed to perfection. But we are learning, and a few years will show a decided improvement. Our climatic conditions are well adapted to poultry raising. With a care to shade and a better understanding of scientific feeding, we will work wonders in a short time.

I have tried mating small pens with an eye especially to the full size of my females, mating to a male rich in color and well marked. Have found the result very satisfactory.

In regard to using males or females with slate in undercolor in order to maintain the markings and black tails, it is still a subject on which we do not all agree, but I have frequently noted that females with slate most frequently have the best marked wings, and by a careful elimination, we can no doubt get good clean undercolored birds. I do not speak with the force of an authority, as it will require a few more years of experimenting before I would venture an opinion along this line, and I hope to see this matter treated by some that have experimented more extensively in this direction.   James M. Frank.

HOW TO GROW RHODE ISLAND RED CHICKS

Artificial Methods Most Satisfactory—Good Wholesome Grain Gives Best Results.

By F. W. HALLETT, Chillicothe, Mo.

In this article I shall confine myself to the rearing of chicks by the artificial method, as we have not used a hen for hatching and brooding the chicks in so long a time, we had really forgotten that this was once a part of her work and give each step as we handle them. Should any one care to follow our method and has chicks from healthy stock, there is no reason for any trouble. We expect some will criticise our method and our feed rations, for we have never had the time to figure out on paper to know if they are balanced according to scientific principles, and somehow we have often wendered if some of the people that claim to know just what a chick needs to produce growth or a hen the egg, have ever really made a success of raising the chicks or getting the eggs. Not long ago an article came to our notice in which the writer claimed that corn should by no means be fed to the laying hen in summer and that whole oats were an injury to them and should only be fed after being hulled. Now I have proven to my own satisfaction that whole oats will increase the egg production right next to green bone and that my hens will sometimes leave wheat or oats to greedily gobble the first bit of cracked corn that strikes the ground. I do not think a chicken, if given a variety and plenty of exercise, will eat too much corn. I would not feed all corn, but wheat, oats and corn and their bi-products are my stand-bys for grains, and for the past seven years my feeding rations have been the same and they are giving me results, and that is all I want. I have also made experiments with different pens of fowls and have found that the above rations give me just as good results as the scientific balanced rations. Give a chicken a chance and he will figure out his own ration properly balanced, and I think better than any one can with a pencil and paper.

We find little chicks hatched from healthy stock pretty hardy little creatures, and if given half a chance and properly cared for will live and grow like little pigs, so to speak; but if neglected, chilled, overfed at the wrong time, I do not know of a more miserable looking creature or a business that will be found more discouraging.

First, we make our own brooders and we lay a part of our success to them; in fact, all the trouble arising from bowel complaints in young chicks from healthy stock we have proven to our own satisfaction at least is caused by two things, viz.: Improper brooders and manner of starting the chicks. Our brooders are of the hot air type with a continuous supply of fresh outside air drawn in around a heater and distributed under the hover on the backs of the chicks. A regulator governs the temperature, and we don't want any brooders in ours that have no regulators. Chicks want an even temperature, and we have no time to sit by and regulate the heat by turning up or down the lamp flame.

Take baby chicks from a temperature of say 103 to 105 degrees in an incubator, place them in a brooder at 95 degrees, and in the morning find the temperature down to 75, or even as low as 65, and the chicks all bunched up to get warm, and in a few days you will see the result— bowel trouble. Another cause for bowel trouble is feeding too quick. Don't feed the chicks for thirty-six hours at the least, 48 hours after hatching is about right, and longer will not hurt them. About the nineteenth day the chicks absorb the yolk, and this alone will keep them alive for five days, so give them a chance to digest this without stuffing them full of other feeds.

We take our chicks from the incubator, place them in lined baskets and cover them up and let them sleep by the warm fire, if in cold weather, for six to twelve hours, putting them in an indoor brooder which has been heated to 100 degrees under the hover two inches from the floor and the floor covered with sand at dark so they cannot see to run around. After the chicks are in we watch the temperature and adjust the regulator to hold at 100 degrees; we turn the regulator a little every night after the chicks are under the hover until we get the heat gradually down to 95 degrees at the end of the first week unless the weather is cold, then we hold at 100 degrees the first week and commence dropping to 95, beginning the second week. In the morning we sprinkle chick grit and chick size charcoal on the brooder floor, give them a fountain of water and leave them to themselves until noon. By this time they have learned the brooder, where the hover is, and we will say, do not place the brooder where the sun can shine in on the floor for the first few days, for you want to teach them that the hover is the place to get warm. If the sun comes in and they find that place, they are likely to be found, huddling there after the sun goes down and will cause you trouble to teach them the hover. By noon they have plenty of grit on the way to the gizzard and their little grist mills will be ready to grind the food that comes. The charcoal will help to keep down any tendency to bowel trouble. By this time they are ready for their first feed, which is bread crumbs dry, and this is given only in small quantities, just what they will clean up in two or three minutes, keeping a supply of grit, charcoal and fresh water always before them. We feed the bread crumbs for the first day, then a feed of chick feed, then bread crumbs, alternating every other feed every two or three hours for about two or three days. On the fourth day we let them into an adjoining part of the brooder which is a large box, the floor of which is covered with short cut alfalfa or chaff from the hay mow. In this litter we scatter the chick feed and make them dig for what they get, also give them a dish of dry mash mixture—bran, shorts and fine corn meal of equal parts by weight, and from now on as long as they are in the brooder we keep this mixture before them. As a night feed we now add hard boiled eggs mixed with fine corn meal, just enough meal to help pulverize the egg feed on boards. The dry mash mixture and the egg feed at night help to keep going any that are slow at learning to dig for the chick feed, which is now fed four or five times a day. We also nail pieces of potatoes to the side of the brooder and hack them with a knife until we get the chicks to pick at them. As soon as one gets to picking the rest soon fall in line, and from now on we feed plenty of potatoes unless we have other greed food. Beginning the middle of the second week we add a hopper of meat meal and discontinue the egg food at night as soon as they get to eating the meat meal readily.

If weather is suitable, beginning the third week we move them to outdoor brooders, moving and tucking them under the hover at night, confine them to the brooder for the first day for them to learn the brooder, then they are given an outside run, which is enlarged as they grow older and learn the way in and out of the brooder. At four weeks of age we mix some whole wheat and cracked corn with the chick feed and gradually wean them from the chick feed to wheat and cracked corn. At five or six weeks old we add a little whole oats, and in a few weeks have them eating whole oats, wheat and cracked corn of equal parts by measure.

We keep them in the brooder until they begin to want to roost on top of the hover and are quite will feathered out. We then move them to large, roomy colony coops that are of the fresh air type with temporary runs for a time until they learn where to come to roost, then they are given range, separating the cockerels from the pullets when placed on range as far as we can tell. The cockerels

SINGLE COMB RHODE ISLAND REDS.

Second pen, Indianapolis, 1909; first pen, Omaha and Kansas City, 1909.   Bred and owned by F. W. Hallett, Chillicothe, Mo.

now receive a hopper of grit, charcoal, meat meal, cracked corn and oats. Pullets receive the same, only we like to feed pullets plenty of wheat, so we add wheat to theirs, and if we are short of wheat, we add the bran, shorts and corn meal mixture which answers the purpose very well. Both cockerels and pullets are kept on range until bad weather in the fall, when we move the pullets to the laying houses. These are of the continuous curtain front type, and curtains are hung on frames hinged to the ceiling and are hooked back and up, leaving the front open except for the wire front, and closed only when stormy and severe cold nights are likely to freeze combs. Some of the cockerels are housed the same way, others are housed in the large colony houses, eight by ten feet. All are given large runs and let out when there is no snow and the weather is suitable.

There are other things we might mention but time will not permit, so we will sum it all down to a few things that poultry need to bring about success: Clean brooders and large, roomy coops, free from lice and mites; plenty of grit, charcoal, grains, fresh water and do not forget the meat food and green food in some form, especially while the chicks are confined to runs around the brooders and brood coops.

Now a few words about the temperature of brooders. Weather conditions vary, so that no rules can be followed successfully. We are of the opinion that some chicks are never kept warm enough. In cold, windy weather we run the heat at 100 degrees under the hover for the first week; when warm or moderate weather, 100 degrees dropped to 95 the end of the first week; hold 95 degrees for about two weeks, then drop to 90 and gradually to about 80 is low enough until they begin to get lots of feathers. The comfort of the chicks is our guide regardless of the temperature of the thermometer. When the chicks are laying flat on the floor with their heads sticking out from under the hover the temperature is right. If no heads are out the chances are that they are cold and are huddling and crowding, which means some of the weaker ones will suffer from being trampled to death. If all are driven out from under the hover and with wings spread out, they are too hot. When the weather is cold at night I like to drive a large percentage out from under the hover early in the evening, then they can have a warmer temperature to run to as the temperature drops along toward morning. Since we have been using plenty of heat, we do not have to throw out from under the hover so many dead chicks in the morning, and when we let them out in the morning there are no three or five that come out all humped up and moving slow like they were about all in. Heat and plenty of it will keep them from crowding and give the weaker ones a chance to grow with the rest. On the other hand, too much heat will weaken the chicks, especially in warm weather; but when it is cold and chilly they will stand a lot of heat. Give them heat and a large, roomy brooder where they can go to the heat or get away from it and they will find what they want. Again, fifty chicks are enough for any brooder. While I sometimes have seventy-five in a bunch, when I have room I like fifty or less number better, for they as a rule grow better. My outdoor brooders are three by six feet, and I have some that are four by eight feet, and fifty to seventy-five is enough for any of them to do the very best.

If this article should be the means of helping anyone to raise to maturity any more of the chicks that are hatched instead of letting them go where so many a once bright and active little bunch of down goes, I shall feel that my time has been well invested.

Popularity of Rhode Island Reds.

At the recent meeting of the Great Mid-West Poultry and Pet Stock Association, the largest and best show ever held in the Coliseum, Chicago, the Rhode Island Reds had the honor of having the largest number of entries.

This has also been true of seven shows I attended the past season. To what can we attribute this record—the fact that our two Red Clubs and every Red breeder is boosting the breed? No. The Reds themselves are responsible for their great popularity; they have forged themselves to the front and are justly entitled to our claims for them, "The best fowl on earth."

The Rhode Island Reds naturally appeal to the fancier. Their great beauty and type is bound to attract attention. Notice at every show the crowds in Red alley. The exhibitors are always busy explaining and showing their birds to enthusiastic buyers, and a canvass after the

show will prove that the breeders in Red alley did more business than the combined sales of any other two breeds.

But while the fanciers are entitled to credit for booming the breed and the reproducing by scientific mating of better Reds, the greatest point in favor of the breed is from the utility standpoint. As an egg machine they have no equal. For market purposes they represent quality. Their yellow legs and skin, medium size, plump, they easily command a premium. For broilers and roasters they are the ideal fowl, as the long body makes the breast exceptionally meaty.

No chick on earth is as easily raised as the Reds. They stand lots of abuse and still thrive and mature early. Chicks hatched in March, April or May are laying by November, and continue through the coldest weather if properly fed and housed.

J. F. MINGEA
OWNER
CHICAGO HEIGHTS, ILL.

Give them a trial and you will always keep them. Start with good stock or eggs and success is assured. At the end of the year you will be a full-fledged "Red crank" and will want to go after the fancy.

Exhibit your best birds and attend the shows. Study the breed. Get a copy of the "Standard of Perfection," join the National Clubs and boost for better Reds.

J. H. Mingea, Chicago Heights, Ill.

What Effect Light or Slate in Undercolor May Have in Offspring.

Light, or white in undercolor I consider one of the most dangerous defects that can be introduced into the breeding yard.

There seems to be two classes of this defect. We find it in birds with excellent surface color and with strong wings and tail. When it appears in this colored bird it usually looks more cottony; it is hard to breed out and should be avoided. It gives an uncertain undercolor and it is next to impossible to breed a good clean, rich undercolor on either male or female.

The very worst form of white in undercolor I consider is where the color is very rich with white on back and saddle, while sometimes extending out from the skin nearly the whole length of feather. The surface color is usually very rich and even, but the tail will be found to be of a russet color and wing markings poor. These birds are sometimes almost free from white as cockerels, but when the cock plumage as finished the true value of the bird is shown.

This defect will produce a weakness in Standard color of offspring; the males will usually all run to red tails and a sort of russet red with white showing in sickles, flight feathers and undercolor. This blood is certain to produce females with no black markings at all, and mealy surface, degenerating to a buff in a couple of generations.

Now, as to slate in undercolor. I do not believe slate is necessary to keep up color when the breeding is handled right. The most important point is the quality of black in the tail and wing. I give the most attention to the male for color. The black should have a green sheen—bottle green, as it is most commonly called—and not a brown sheen. A male with such quality of black is always loaded with value for color breeding; provided of course, that he is of even surface and bright red. The best Reds of both sexes I ever produced were red from just such a male. I mated this bird with four pullets of rich even red color, but not real strong in black markings, with the result that their offspring won the most important prizes in such wonderful classes of Reds as were brought together at Chicago, Buffalo, Youngstown, Indianapolis, Toronto, Cleveland, etc.

LADY ARISTOCRAT.

Bred and owned by Ira M. Crowthers, Willoughby, Ohio.

My International Champion pullet at the Buffalo show was from this mating. Her color was a bright live red, one shade all over, so even that it could hardly be seen where one feather began and another left off. The males were of the same quality of color exactly; extremely live, rich red, that shown out with brilliancy and lustre entirely free from that bronzing and russet color.

When color is running toward a mealy brown and weak black sections, I am sure there is no quicker or safer way to strengthen that flock than to use a male with the right quality of black in tail and wing with a slight barr of slate on back in undercolor. It will in most cases give instant relief. The surface color of offspring will take on new life at once, and right here I want to say use new blood every time, and I would use it through the male, as I consider better, more speedy results are obtained in color breeding.

I consider undercolor a very important matter in breeding Reds. It must have character, that is, bright live red.

In summing up finally, look to the male to do more than his half in color breeding; be sure he has the correct bottle green sheen in tail, and an even bright red surface and use him with or without a little bar of slate, according to the extent of the rundown condition of color in your own strain; always remembering that your color will degenerate into a buff or russet, unless birds of the correct quality of color both in red and black are used in your breeding yards.

Ira M. Crowther,

Breeder of the Famous "Aristocrat" S. C. Reds. Willoughby, Ohio.

ARISTOCRAT.

The male that founded the famous strain of S. C. Reds. Owned and bred by Ira M. Crowthers, Willoughby, Ohio.

Mating and Rearing Rhode Island Reds.

Yours requesting an article on mating Rhode Island Reds, and rearing the chicks was duly received, and I had intended to answer same promptly, but when I tried to think what I knew along those lines it seemed to me that everyone in the poultry business knew it as well as myself, and there are a number who have just started in the work who know a great deal more than I, or in fact any of the old breeders do about Rhode Island Reds, and they publish whole books of literature on these subjects.

Under these conditions it seems rather presumptious on my part to attempt to say much. I have bred pure bred fowls since 1867, including many varieties.

MO-HAWK.

First prize winner, Detroit, January 9-14, 1909. Owned by I. A. Sibley, South Bend, Ind.

My father-in-law, Mr. Seir Curtis, of Buffalo, N. Y., was a charter member of the American Poultry Association, and I was present at its formation, and should have been a member but for the fact that I was then a traveling salesman, and my territory was Minnesota, too far away from the "then" centre of the poultry boosters. I have also been a breeder of horses and cattle during all of these years, and quite a close observer of conditions.

My experience, as well as my observations, have taught me that like produces like, or the likeness of some "great" ancestor. I emphasize the word "great," because I mean just what the word implies. This great ancestor must be great in all ways, strong physically, in fact so much of an "individual" as to stamp his progeny with the likeness of himself. This rule applies to the breeding of everything from the human being down to chickens.

For this reason, I would rather have a well bred bird, from yards with established lines of breeding (always providing that those established lines were those which I desire to get), which would not score so high as some bird of unknown breeding with a high mark.

In breeding Rhode Island Reds, I always try to bear in mind the thing which makes them valuable and which has brought them to the front so rapidly, and that is their utility qualities; in other words, egg production and table quality and quantity.

In regard to mating birds, we prefer to mate cockerels with hens, and cock birds with pullets. In our best pens we mate up those birds which are as nearly perfect as possible, both males and females. Last season over sixty per cent. of the birds from our best matings scored better than 90.

If our females were inclined to be too light in color we would try to mate them to a cockerel with an excess of dark pigment in his color, and would not object to some smut in under color or some dark feathers in the wing bows. If, on the other hand, our females were inclined to have too much slate or smut in undercolor, we would try to mate them to a male bird with as bright a red color as possible, uniform in color from head to tail, and we would not be over particular about the wing markings in this male.

The male contributes fifty per cent. of the blood lines

of the flock, and with care in his selection one can build up his flock rapidly. In asking for quotations on birds, it would be a great help to the one from whom you make inquiry as well as a benefit to yourself, if you would say just along what lines you wish to make improvement, what faults you wish to overcome.

Every honest breeder is anxious that his customers shall get good results with the stock which he sends them, and will always try to send such birds as he believes will accomplish this.

Finally, kill every bird which you do not think is good enough to breed to, or if you wish to keep them for winter layers, keep them separated from those few choice ones which you have selected for breeders, and save your eggs for hatching from those selected birds properly mated. Send some of your best ones to the poultry show, and go yourself. No matter whether you win or not, you will learn a great deal at the show and go home better prepared for the next year's work. If you attend the large shows, you will meet some of the brightest men and women in the world—people from every walk in life, doctors, lawyers, bankers, ministers, merchants, farmers and their wives—all interested in and getting enjoyment, profits and recreation out of the chickens, and you will find such a spirit of good fellowship prevailing that you will want to go again.

In regard to raising the little chicks, we hatch most of our birds in incubators, raise them in brooders, give them plenty of good green grass to run on, keep their quarters scrupulously clean, feed mostly of prepared chick foods, together with some fresh chopped beef (hamburger steak), hard boiled eggs, and of course always supplying plenty of grit, oyster shells and charcoal. A bountiful supply of fresh water is of great importance both to old and young birds.

For the baby chicks we prepare the water which is given to them by adding three drops each of carbolic acid and tincture of iron to the pint of water the first day, adding one drop of each each day until we reach six drops of

MIN-NE-HA-HA.

First prize winner, Chicago, December 16-19, 1908; Detroit, January 9-14, 1909. Owned by I. A. Sibley, South Bend, Ind.

each to the pint of water, at which point we continue until the chicks are half to two-thirds grown.

The carbolic acid and tincture of iron is for the purpose of destroying intestinal worms, which cause the death of so many young chicks. These may be readily recognized in the little chicks by the feathers sticking out, the heads becoming peaked and the wings drooping. Since learning the use of this in the water, we have lost less than 5 per cent. of the chicks hatched. The production of the best specimens depends as much upon the raising as upon the breeding.   Yours most truly,

Irving A. Sibley,
South Bend, Ind.

"The Rhode Island Red of the Future."

As a breeder of Rhode Island Reds, I derive great pleasure in helping to advance a breed which so completely fills the needs of both utility breeder and fancier.

Well do I remember several years ago, when I expressed to a prominent poultryman my intention of giving the S. C. Reds a trial, he made sport of me and remarked that they were only scrubs and that I would be wasting time. I carried my plans into effect, and the first year's trial convinced me that they were the best utility fowl, at least, that I had ever had experience with, and from year to year I have grown stronger in the belief. For the first two years I only bred for utility purposes, but was all the while breeding for a type that I thought desirable and which type today is helping me to win in the big shows.

I soon found they were improving in color and I began to be interested from the fancier's standpoint, and it has been very gratifying to me to see the wonderful advance-

classes. While I hardly get an entire flock of hens of the same bright color as the pullets, for it is a difficult proposition with a plumage containing so much coloring matter as the best specimens of Reds do, I have seen a few hens with color almost equal to the best pullets and expect to breed many of them of such qualifications in the course of a few years.

The wing markings on females are coming nicely, and we can soon find the plain winged female the uncommon specimen rather than the strong winged specimen as at present.

There is a tendency toward a striped hackle in many individuals, and I might say in many flocks of Reds, but by exercising great care in our mating it can be overcome. The past season I produced a number of pullets with fine wing markings, and yet in hackle they only have the Standard ticking, so I feel sure this can be accomplished, yet do not think it probable that we could ever get a good wing on the larger percentage of females if we were to eliminate all black from the hackle. Another point in

SINGLE COMB RHODE ISLAND REDS.
First Pen at Indianapolis, 1909. Bred and owned by B. H. Scranton, Rising Sun, Ind.

ment we, as breeders, have made in our choice of all breeds. It is a conceded fact that no breed has made such remarkable strides to perfection in the past few years as have the Reds.

But, what of the future? Can we expect as great progress toward the Standard in the next five years as the past five years have brought about? There is no question but what if we continue with careful, consistent matings, that there will be equally as much improvement. The time is not far away when our flocks of Reds will be as uniform as any other breed.

I can see in my own yards that the birds average a much higher percentage of high class birds than they did even one year ago. We will always find a slight difference in the shade of red in the individual birds, but the extremely light birds and those with uneven and mottled surface colors will soon be uncommon.

I expect to see a very great improvement in our hen

which I hope to see a great change; that is, in the evenness of surface color of the male birds. There is too much contrast in the larger percentage of the males of today. The hackle, wing bows and saddle are of different shades of red, which spoils the appearance of the bird.

It is the blending of color that makes the Red male bird so beautiful, and along this line I expect to work and accomplish a great change. We can find some specimens that are practically one shade now, but they are the exception and not the rule.

There is a tendency among some breeders, and judges as well, to favor the very dark bird. This is desirable only to a degree. We get them so dark we lose that rich, brilliant lustre so pleasing to the eye and instead have a brown which does not permit of the brilliancy we can get in a bird of the medium dark color. I think there is no doubt but that Reds will average a little darker in the future than they have in the past, but great care must be exercised to avoid this very dark shade of undesirable color.

We have found too many bad combs among the Reds of both combs, but here is where we can expect a marked improvement the coming seasons as they are very much better in this section than a few years ago. We will see them in the near future averaging as good in comb as the best flocks of Rocks or Wyandottes.

But to the most important point and one which must not be lost sight of—this is type. The Standard has given us a type of bird such that the carcass measurements if bred up to give us the greatest utility fowl on earth.

This distinction the Reds have already attained and I see no reason why we should lay down the title to another breed. Let us ever keep in mind that long, deep body and not allow ourselves to sacrifice this for the sake of desirable color alone. These shape requirements should always be uppermost in the mind of the Red breeder and if so the Reds can not help but continue to grow in popularity in the future as in the past. Summing it all up I feel safe in predicting that the Reds, as a flock, will in the future come as near complying with the Standard requirements as set for by the American Poultry Association as any of the older breeds.

With such an earnest, enthusiastic association of breeders who do things, I can picture nothing but the brightest future for our favorites.

B. H. Scranton,
Rising Sun, Ind.

Disadvantages of More Than One Club.

The question is frequently asked nowadays, "Are the specialty clubs becoming too numerous?"

So far as Rhode Island Reds are concerned, I am confident that the three clubs will tend to weaken rather than strengthen the popularity of the breed. That is a broad and, you may think, a bold assertion, but a careful analysis of the field today and the breed as we find it confirms me in the opinion.

Take the color of the Rhode Island Red. Red is not a fixed or absolutely known color to each and every eye, like white or black. When you say "red" to an average ten people, a different mind picture or ideal of red will come to the minds of nearly the entire number. One auditor will call up a vision of brilliant cherry red (and even cherry red may have different shades), and another will call up a deep rich garnet red, a third will see a mixture or blending of the two, and so on. You may take five selected shades of red and put them before five different people and ask them to pick out the ideal red as described in our Standard of Perfection and the chances are that no two will agree on the shade. The color of the Rhode Island Red then is to many people an unfixed color. This being so, I regard it as very important that the club-work for the breed be directed by one club alone. Why? Because with two or three clubs, there is much danger that a division will arise over this color, or rather shade question. One club is likely to teach that a certain shade is the ideal color while another club will hold to a different shade. The officers of a specialty club are supposed to be experts in the characteristics of the breed the club seeks to promote. If two specialty clubs for the same breed have officers that teach different colors, the confusion will grow worse instead of better in Red circles. To my mind this is a strong reason why we should have only one club, so that one ideal of color may be fixed and work toward harmony.

The shape of the Red is also a knotty question with many breeders. Wyandotte and Rock types pass current with too many breeders as the ideal. With two or three clubs the same danger as in color arises—different teachings by the different clubs.

It may be argued that the different clubs are for promoting the variety, as single and rose combs. That is true. But should not the rose and single comb have the same color and the same shape? Most assuredly. Then does not the danger increase when you set up different clubs with different types and colors perhaps? In a word, there is more danger of two sets of officers and two sets of executive committee men working toward different ideals than there is of one set. The danger increases even more rapidly when you tack on the third club.

Then the time comes, when the American Poultry association will be consulting the specialty clubs for suggestions about color, shape and other characteristics. Unless unity of action among the breeders is secured through a good strong club, the best interests of the breed will suffer. If two, or worse, three clubs go before the association with different types and different shades of color, then the best interests of the breed will surely suffer. History of breeds little bred now will show that here have been danger points that the breed failed to get by. A breed may be "clubbed" to death very easily here.

Another thing, with one club only, you have a larger fund to use in offering cups and specials. Unquestionably more breeders will join one big booming live club than will pay three dollars into three weak, sniveling, insignificant clubs. The breeder knows that in union is strength and he wants to get in among that strength.

While it is true that every one doesn't "follow the crowd," yet it is well to have the crowd along, and you will get nearly every thing going. The bigness of a club is an excellent advertisement for not only the club, but the breed.

Rhode Island Reds differ in many respects from the other breeds. Being a new breed, comparatively, to the fanciers over a good part of the country, their characteristics are not so well known as some other breeds. It is therefore, as formerly pointed out, important that one guiding idea prevail along disputed lines of type and color. During the past year it was my pleasure to be in many of the leading show rooms of the country. Reds were shown in them from practically every quarter of America. The greatest complaint I heard against Reds from their severest critics was the lack of uniformity in type and color. Frankness compels me to say that this complaint is not without a foundation. It is not confined to any one section. I saw as many birds I thought too dark at Madison Square as I did at Kansas City. I saw as many birds too light, as I thought, at one show as at another. In a word, the color and type are not altogether a fixed idea in any one section. The danger of different type and different color shades are the two rocks that will be the wreck of the Reds unless carefully guided by one club.

My own individual idea is that the Rhode Island Red Club of America, having originated in the same clime as the birds themselves, and having so wonderfully brought the birds to popularity in so short a time, should still be entrusted with the guiding care of the breed yet in the formative stage.

So give us one good strong club. Let that club push the work of securing members in every part of the country. Let cups be offered wherever the members of that state desire. Every breeder get behind and boost. It has been predicted that the Reds would go the way of the other breeds, but the breed not only has superior merit but also had, and we believe will still have, proper advertising of its merits to a public that wants the best.

Reese V. Hicks, In Red Hen Tales.

THE MOST POPULAR BREED EVER ORIGINATED

By C. L. BUSCHMAN, Originator of Non-Fading Rose Comb Rhode Island Reds.

The fancier or farmer desiring to breed thorough-bred poultry for pleasure or profit, or both, should just study which breed or variety appeals most to his eye. He may chose white, black, or colored fowl. A white bird is very pretty on the farm, but is easily distinguished by hawks. In the city they become soiled and do not have the pretty appearance they should have. Nothing is more distressing to the real lover of poultry than a soiled or bedraggled fowl. Then, if your fancier deals in fine bred, pedigreed stock, he must wash every high-priced bird sent out, or which enters

"TRILBY."

First pullet at Indianapolis, February, 1909, and color special. Produced 102 eggs in 131 days; dam of King Philip, Jr., and other noted winners. C. L. Buschmann, Indianapolis, Ind.

the show room. Only those who have been through conditioning a string of white birds for the show room would know the hours of hard work this means, as well as the chance you run of your birds contracting a severe cold and perhaps dying on your hands.

The black fowl does fairly well in the city, but when dressed for the table makes a poor appearance indeed. People like a yellow skinned bird. They are also very tedious to pick the black pin feathers from.

Partly for these reasons people over the United States have cast an eye upon the Reds, and once given a chance, they win their way to the heart of every true fancier. There never has been a bird admitted to the Standard that has grown so fast in popularity and improved so much in quality as have the Rhode Island Reds. Those of the fanciers who have bred Barred Rocks, Wyandottes, Leghorns, etc., and who have bred a few of the Reds at the same time, for the sake of comparison, are becoming convinced that Rhode Island Reds have not a rival as a layer and table fowl combined.

The bird is of purely American origin, and we believe is the most profitable fowl raised today. They are hearty, vigorous, and great foragers. The also do well in confinement. For beauty we believe there is none which surpasses them and as an all-around layer, they are unequaled. We have a large number of birds in our breeding yards to-

day that have laid seventy-five to ninety eggs in the last hundred days. Every bird is banded, trap nests are used, and an accurate record kept of each hen's egg production. This is the only fair way that such a record can be taken, and it lays the foundation for your best.

A few years ago people would say Rhode Island Reds would be all right if the hens did not fade, and look so bad after moulting. We have had hundreds of breeders of Rhode Island Reds visit our yards in the past spring that said they never saw such beautiful hens and did not think that it was possible to raise Rhode Island Reds that would not fade.

This we started out to accomplish, and we feel that we have made rapid strides and great progress along this line. We have birds today three and four years old that have the beautiful color of the pullet and still they go right on producing the eggs just the same as the faded out birds, that are found in the yards of many breeders. Some of these claimed that the fading out of the birds was convincing evidence that they were great layers. This has been proved untrue by our trap nested records, the kind of birds we have shown, and those to be found in our yards today.

"KING PHILIP"
FIRST PRIZE COCK, CHICAGO DEC. 1909.
OWNED AND BRED BY ... C. L. BUSCHMAN, INDIANAPOLIS, IND.

In every village, township, county and State there is an opportunity for a good Rhode Island Red business. Start a pen of well-bred Reds from a setting of eggs, or by purchasing a pen. Advertising is not absolutely necessary; your neighbors will soon learn about your Reds and will want a few settings. Others will hear of it and soon you will supply a large quantity of eggs throughout your county.

Next, exhibit your birds at your local show or fair. Learn the good points and talk them up. In another year it will take all your efforts to supply the demand. Make up more pens, get new blood, establish line breeding, advertise, and you soon become a "big man" in the Rhode Island Red business, with both pleasure and profit for your small investment.

JUST A WORD ABOUT BREEDING

LESTER TOMPKINS, in Red Hen Tales.

I have been asked to write an article on mating Rhode Island Reds. While my experience with this breed covers about thirty-seven years, I am still trying to produce better birds each season. As to being authority on "Scientific Mating," I am far from that.

Some of the experienced fanciers who have, within a few years, taken some of the best specimens, the results of years of outcrossing, should be able to give more satisfactory information than myself, as I am only a farmer and bred them originally wholly for utility, only breeding for fancy stock for about ten years, and am still maintaining the farm flock with the old-time vigor.

I have to smile when I hear some of our leading admirers and fanciers speak of the Rhode Island Reds as a comparatively new breed. I suppose it is a little different with me from most breeders, as this breed is the first fowl I ever knew. Forty years ago we saw them in every farmer's barnyard, through Little Compton, R. I., which place was my native town. This fowl also could be found in Westport, the adjoining town. I might say that I was born and brought up with these birds, having them for playthings when a mere child. In those days, when hatched early in the spring, the young chicks were brought into the kitchen for a few days, and we children found great amusement in feeding them. My father bought poultry for New Bedford, Newport, New York and Boston markets from that particular part of Rhode Island from which nearly all the best poultry was to be found in those days. The name of Rhode Island poultry still lives in these same markets today as being best quality.

When a small boy, before going to school, I used to ride with father collecting and buying from the farmers. This brought me in touch with all the flocks through that section. Father being a born poultryman, we always looked for the best birds, and when we would see a good specimen along the roadside, we commented on the qualities. When I grew older and had chickens of my own, I always experimented each year by selecting best specimens from the flock and mating them to see what they would produce. It was very interesting to watch the results and I am still interested in the same way, trying to improve each year.

Now as to proper mating to produce ideal birds, it is the old story in a measure, that like produces like, but, as in other breeds, it is safer to know your blood lines and what is back of the birds to be mated. To a beginner: —In selecting hens, which I like best, as breeders, you are very apt to be deceived in your bird, as many of them that were good color as pullets, and are many times best breeders and producers of good stock, you would not take a second look at in regard to mating to produce fine stock, as they have been through a heavy season of laying. As they are such phenomenal layers the strain on the system takes the life from the color of the plumage, which makes it light or faded. Still the constitution and bodily health has such vigor, they can stand the wear and tear and will produce good stock. Of course, if we have one that

will go through and still hold her color, I prize that kind very highly. Then look out for the hen that shows up fine, that as a pullet was a scrub, they are many times worse than useless in the breeding pen. To the female we look for shape, size and Rhode Island Red character. Now, after you have selected your **female** that has good shape and as good head points as possible, we come to the **male** on which we depend mostly for color and stamina, while a great deal depends upon surface color as that is always in sight. Still I think undercolor quite important as to breeding qualities. It may not always be the cleanest, purest colored, or the darkest colored, but strength and richness is important. Don't mistake my meaning as to strength and richness, as it is not always the darkest bird that is the richest. If a dark bird has pure undercolor and brilliant surface color, very good. Sometimes a rather lightish male that is rich and bred from a dark bird, makes the best breeder.

AVOID: Extremes in color between male and female. If, as many say, my pullets are a little light in color, it is safer to darken color by degrees than to attempt doing it all in one season by using an extremely dark male, as this is one of the causes of unevenness in the flock.

Line breeding, when properly carried out, is all right for bringing out certain requirements and fixing some of the points desired, but one should thoroughly understand line breeding, and Rhode Island Red characteristics before attempting it to a very great degree, as this breed was made up by outcrossing for many years. Do not mistake line breeding with in breeding.

It is a well known fact that Rhode Island Reds are the results of from sixty to seventy years or more of outcrossing and has been one of the main factors in producing great strength and strong constitution and laying qualities which are some of the principal points that have brought the Rhode Island Reds to the present popularity. This feature cannot be overlooked, to maintain **ruggedness**, but, the same as in line breeding, one must be careful, as it is important that you know the line you are using for this purpose.

While the Reds are a very old breed as bred by the Rhode Island farmer, but very few fanciers have bred them many years, and one taking farm stock to start with must not expect to breed out undesirable qualities in a minute. My advice is: Go slowly with farm-bred stock until you know their characteristics, as they vary on different farms. Some farmers fancied one shade of cream white, while another a different one, but all were after laying qualities and poultry.

Select birds for outcrossing from such strain, if they can be found, that have been bred on the same line for a number of generations. The best results I ever obtained in a single season was from some females I got from an old farmer that bred them carefully for years without new blood. While they were not show birds, they were strong in some of the requirements of the Rhode Island Red standard. These females were mated with one of my own line bred males and that had been line bred carefully for ten years or more, the union of these two strong bloods brought great results.

I think these points must be considered in maintaining the old-time vigor and hardiness of the breed. We often hear those good old-fashioned Red birds spoken of, which I believe can be produced today as good and better, if one will stop and think. Get the old-fashioned type as we call it, fixed in your mind, then learn the true color and stick to it, but don't take birds that were produced by accident and expect to breed standard birds in one season.

Rhode Island Reds as They Grow

During the Buffalo show, in January, 1910, the editor had a long visit with George W. Tracy, well known to the Rhode Island Red fraternity in the Eastern and Middle States. Mr. Tracy had just completed a visit of nearly all the prominent Red farms in New York and the New England States. Knowing him to be one of the closest observers of the breed we had met, I asked him for some information about several of the yards he had visited. Our conversation was constantly broken into by friends of one or the other of us that we had not met for some time, shaking hands and passing the time of day, but I learned enough from Mr. Tracy to know that an article from him describing just what he had found in the several breeders' yards would be interesting reading, and we arranged with him to tell the readers of this book in his own way just where he found the good ones, and if possible to give the ancestors of several birds that we had handled during the past two years.

Following is the article just as it came from Mr. Tracy's pen. Every breeder who has produced the good ones found by Mr. Tracy is named and full credit given him, and we feel that the readers will find much that will interest them in the following pages.   Editor.

RHODE ISLAND REDS AS I HAVE FOUND THEM

With Full Credit to All Breeders, Who Have Produced Individuals From Which Prominent Strains Were Established.

By GEORGE W. TRACY, Kinderhook, N. Y.

Mr. Hewes requested me to give to the readers of his new book on Rhode Island Reds my impressions of the various flocks of Reds as I found them upon the farms or in the yards of the numerous breeders that it has been my pleasure and profit to visit. His idea is for me to present the Reds as they appear, comparing them with the other popular breeds, both as to general looks as a flock, as well as their comparative worth as to the utility qualities.

Always a "chicken crank," as lovers of poultry are dubbed, I took up the Reds. I bred them for a time and liked them. As they grew in popularity, I became inoculated with the germ of the showing bug. This germ was nurtured by the glowing reports of the wonderful victories that my friend, J. Frank Van Alstyne, had achieved with his world renowned Silver Wyandottes. I had a sneaking notion that I might cut as wide a swath with my Reds, but I first made up my mind that I would see what the other fellows had and showed. This led to my visiting various poultry shows and also visiting prominent breeders of Reds, then becoming connected with poultry journalism in the capacity of an associate editor and a field representative, or in other words visiting breeders with the view of securing advertising for the paper I represented. This gave me wonderful opportunities to view innumerable numbers of Reds, but I also was in a position to compare them with other breeds or varieties that I saw upon the different plants and farms that I visited. When I made my first trip, several years ago, my fame as a poultry breeder had gotten no further than my own vicinity, hence I was taken for a man that was looking up something that I had but very little knowledge of, but it was very fruitful of results to me, as I found every breeder of Reds courteous and willing to show me their birds and also give the results of their experience with mating and breeding.

One of the earliest criticisms of the Reds was that while they looked well in a coop in the show room, the flocks as found on the different farms didn't in any way compare with the birds on exhibition. The same can be truthfully said of any of the other popular breeds; take the Barred Rock for example. In the show room you will see a number of birds all of very nearly the same color. On the majority of farms you will see them of different, very different, shades of color—some females almost black and some of the males almost white. You will read of the White Wyandotte as the bird of graceful curves and snowy white plumage, and beautiful pictures are often drawn of green, shady lawns, dotted here and there with beautiful birds of snowy whiteness, often being likened to the color of the driven snow; but alas, how different in real life, and how often do you see whole flocks of white birds, whose plumage is the color of the snow that you will see in the back yard after it has been treated with coats of dish-water, pails of ashes, etc. They surely don't always show the immaculate whiteness of the show room, nor could it be expected. Here is where I am going to state that the Red is the greatest breed of them all to conceal dirt. They may have plenty of it on them, but they don't show; hence, if they do fade, they still preserve their good looks.

I am writing now from experience gained in the manner before stated. When I started to visit Rhode Island Red poultry farms, I started high, as the very first one I visited was Lester Tompkins's. He was just dressing to go to Boston as a witness in a horse case. He said I could go along or else stay and look at the stock until he came back. I chose to go along, as a horse case is always interesting, and, strange to relate, at Mr. Tompkins's suggestion, I was placed on the stand, and I was able to discredit the testimony of the other side, in so far as the value of the horse

was concerned. They tried to show that the mare was valuable, especially for breeding; as she was subject to quarter cracks, my testimony tended to show that she was worthless on account of her feet, as she would be certain to transmit her weakness to her offspring. This is digressing, but I could scarcely refrain from mentioning it as it was certainly peculiar that I should leave my New York State home to study Reds and be called to the witness stand in the great city of Boston. The opposing lawyer asked me if I was a veterinary surgeon. I answered, "No, simply a common horse shoer." It was a novel experience for me, and I enjoyed the discomfiture of the opposing lawyer, as he wasn't up much on horses' feet. Our lawyer appeared to know something, as I had tutored him up as to the questions he should ask me.

After the trial we traveled back to Concord and I spent several days looking over Mr. Tompkins's stock. Mr. Tompkins is probably the oldest breeder (not in age) of Reds in the country. His version of his connection with them was that his father bred them exclusively, and when he purchased his present home in Concord, he brought some of his father's stock with him and only bred them for utility purposes. He didn't call himself a fancier, but, happening to visit the Boston show, and in looking over the Reds, he offered to wager a goodly sum that he could pick a string from his flock that would beat the whole Red exhibit in the show. The next year he began showing his birds, and the whole world knows the result. I made a careful study of Mr. Tompkins's pens and his methods of mating. The visit of which I am writing was after his first big winning at New York, and as it was about the first week in April, I saw the pens as they were mated up for the season. His flock consisted of about 1,100 females and, take them all in all, they would compare favorably in looks with any similar-sized flock of any other variety. The male birds were all of a rich, lustrous shade of red, and as it was in the spring, the pullets had held their color, while the yearlings and over, if they had faded or come in lighter, their splendid shape and hardy, healthy looks made the flock as a whole handsome to behold. He had some females seven and eight years old, and from a pen of these aged hens, mated with a dark, even colored young cockerel, the first pen pullets of the next winter at New York were produced. In all my readings on poultry, I don't recollect of reading that this pullet or hen is a perfect picture of her father. While at a certain big show last fall, a certain exhibitor made a big winning on a pullet and cockerels. He was an honest man, as can be judged by his saying to me, "Every cockerel and pullet that I won on in this show are from eggs I purchased from Lester Tompkins, and birds from my own stock got nothing." We were looking at his winning pullet. She was a dandy. I said "I'll bet you I can tell you what bird she is out of." "Which one?" said he. I answered, "The cockerel that won first and champion challenge cup at Boston." "How do you know?" I answered, "She looks just like him." "Well, you are right. I bought two settings of his $25.00 eggs and these birds are all from them." So, high as the eggs were, he made money on them, as he sold the pullet for a big price and she won first at a great Western show, and I saw her do it.

Yes, I met a good many that told me that they got their start from Lester Tompkins. Besides being strictly show birds, the Tompkins strain are utility birds, as he is able to sell eggs in large numbers the year around. His houses are modest structures, not a whole lot of money invested in them. They are rather of the colony order, but they seem to be just right, as his flock always seems healthy. Mr. Tompkins's business is immense, always having at least two assistants besides his son. His daughter helps with the correspondence and Mrs. Tompkins also does her share. Mr. Tompkins never has used an incubator. All his hatching thus far has been with hens, so it is easy for him to tell the breeding of his birds. Mr. Tompkins's sales last year footed up to over $10,000—quite a sum. No wonder he likes Reds!

Frank D. Read, of Fall River, Massachusetts, has a little yard back of his store. It is here that he keeps the pens that lay the eggs that hatch many winning Single Comb Rhode Island Reds. Frank is still a young man, but he is an old fancier. He bred prize winning Barred Rocks, but jumped to the Reds about twelve years ago. He is a very particular breeder. I have visited his place a number of times and I never saw anything but a show bird in his pens, and any visitor will go away satisfied with Reds after viewing Frank's flock, as every bird on his place is red. His strain is noted for the many fine females that have sprung from it. Frank informed me that he bred Reds for several years, but he got his real start when he purchased a cockerel from a Mr. Allen, of Apponaug, Rhode Island. This bird is the foundation of Mr. Read's present strain. Mr. Allen created quite a furore some years ago by the superior Single Comb Reds that he showed. Many breeders secured some of his choice specimens and the birds thus secured laid the foundation for many a noted strain of Reds, and while Mr. Allen is comparatively unknown to our latter day breeders, many of his old-time customers are famous the country over, and are known as our very best breeders. Frank C. Read is one of them. Public and luck play no part in his success. Year after year his matings produce many high quality exhibition birds, thus attesting to his skill as a breeder of Rhode Island Reds.

It will be a great revelation to the American Poultry Public to learn that the blood of House Rock Poultry Farm Reds, both Rose and Single Comb, plays a very, very important part in the make-up of some of the very best Rhode Island Reds ever produced. All the world knows that Hon. C. M. Bryant, President of the American Poultry Association, is an enthusiastic Red man, but the extreme modesty of the man has hidden his true position, as the real, living pioneer breeder and staunch advocate of the American truly national breed. When his attention was called to the Reds as a breed, he secured some of the best specimens of the Macomber birds. These were Rose Combs. Mr. Bryant bred them together and improved them. He furnished the late lamented Robert Tuttle with both stock and eggs from his birds of this noted strain and the stock and eggs thus furnished were the foundation of the greatest and most remarkable strain of Rose Combs ever produced from the eggs furnished by Mr. Bryant, Mr. Tuttle's famous St. Louis, Boston and New York winning hen, and to the blood of this remarkable female, Mr. Tuttle attributed the wonderful color of the many great birds produced by Mr. Tuttle and by the various breeders that had secured either stock or eggs from Mr. Tuttle. I always wondered where Mr. Tuttle first got his start for his strain. I first obtained an inkling of it at one of the executive committee meetings at Boston. Mr. Tuttle afterwards confirmed my suspicions by telling me the truth about his strain and I afterwards learned from Mr. Bryant where he secured the stock that produced the birds and laid the eggs that he sold Mr. Tuttle, and when Mr. Tuttle wanted some new blood, he paid Mr. Bryant $150.00 for the cockerel that won first at Boston in 1908, but in giving credit to Mr. Bryant, does not detract one iota from Robert Tuttle's great fame as a breeder. As Frank D. Read perfected a wonderful strain from the descendant's of the cockerel he purchased from Mr. Allen, so Mr. Tuttle, with the aid of the Macomber blood secured from Hon. C. M. Bryant, originated a strain of birds, the most potent in the history of American poultry. We visited Mr. Tuttle quite frequently and we gained a mint of knowledge from an examination of his matings. Mr. Tuttle never kept what you would call a large flock. He generally mated up about twelve pens and each pen was selected as to color. It was always a great treat to view his breeding pens and, like Frank Read's, show birds predominated and visitors always left Mr. Tuttle's place thoroughly satisfied that Reds, such as Mr. Tuttle showed them were marvels of beauty and were strikingly handsome as a flock.

Col. Bryant also helped another breeder onto the road to fame. This breeder, not being overburdened with this world's goods, paid Mr. Bryant $1.50 a piece for fourteen (14) Single Comb pullets. He originally intended, and so bargained to send this breeder some nice, big early hatched pullets that came a little off in color (a good many used to come that way in the old days), but when he came to send the birds, he changed his mind and very generously sent this innocent young amateur breeder younger pullets, but of a far better quality. One of these pullets was later

awarded first at Madison Square Garden. She, in turn, produced some fine females, one of which won special for best shaped female at the Great Chicago show, and this season seven of her great-granddaughters were among the Single Comb winners at the last Madison Square Garden show. Four of them were in a pen and three of them were among the single winners; namely, 1st, 2d and 5th. This is a performance that may never again be equaled. When I arrived at Wollaston, before calling on Mr. Bryant, I learned a few things about him. One of them was that he was a mighty hard man to beat in anything he undertakes, especially when he is a candidate for office. Wollaston is a part of the city of Quincy, Mass., noted in history as being the home of John Adams and his son, John Quincy Adams, two of our early Presidents. Quincy is ordinarily Democratic, but when things get so they need purifying or straightening out, the Independents trot out Col. Bryant, run him for Mayor, and although a Republican, triumphantly elect him, and he always has given a fine business administration. This is the kind of a man that is at the helm in the American Poultry Association. Colonel Bryant has done a lot for the Reds, more than any single man. Since his election to the presidency of the A. P. A. he hasn't been much in the public eye as a breeder, not doing any advertising to speak of, as he didn't wish to profit by the exalted position he occupies in the A. P. A., but he has some very nice Reds, all the same, and I forgot to mention that Mr. Bryant's strain of Single Combs were also of the Allen stock. Mr. Bryant is one of New England's leading business men.

I. W. Bean, of South Braintree, Mass., is the best exclusive Rose Comb Rhode Island Red breeder the country affords, and no doubt it will be interesting to our brother Red men to learn how he got started on the road to success. To begin with, we will say that Mr. Bean is a man of considerable intelligence and business capacity, and it takes that kind to succeed. He bred Single Comb Reds for a great number of years, and in 1901 he purchased two settings of Rose Comb eggs from Mr. P. R. Park, of Park & Pollard, of Boston, from which he raised the celebrated cock bird, "Dictator." The next year he purchased two pullets from H. W. Savage, one of which he has to this day, and at seven years of age is still hale and hearty. This hen is still red and is a great breeder, and every daughter from her is a great breeder, and the union of "Dictator" males with old "Granny," as she is named, females, mingled with an infusion of Tuttle blood, has made the celebrated Bean Strain of Rose Comb Reds. He purchased six settings of eggs from Mr. Tuttle one year, and all he raised from the six settings that he cared to use was one cockerel. This cockerel wasn't good enough to show, but mated with some of the Dictator-Granny cross females, he produced some birds that he used to perfect his strain, the Tuttle color nicking with the Dictator-Granny stock, which had size and shape as well as strong wing markings. Mr. Tuttle's birds had become a little undersized, so much so that it caused him no little concern, and seeing the necessity of doing something to remedy this, and knowing Mr. Bean's strain had some of his blood in their make-up, he secured several females of Mr. Bean's strain, mated them with the first New York and Boston cockerel (1909), and from this union produced the first Chicago cockerel, also first Chicago and Boston pen. The first Chicago cockerel was second to Mr. Bean's great cockerel at Boston. Mr. Bean has done the Rose Comb cause a great service. When he started with them, the Rose Combs, as a rule, were Wyandotty in type, but great improvement has been manifested of late.

Here again is an instance of the influence of the McComber blood secured by President Bryant. The Tuttle strain owes its great color to the blood of the wonderful old New York, Boston and St. Louis first prize hen. She was hatched from eggs sold Mr. Tuttle by Mr. Bryant. Mr. Bryant produced the birds that laid the eggs from his judicious mating of the McComber birds he so fortunately secured and Mr. Bean's strain, splendid as it was, owes its splendid present perfection to the scientific infusion of the old Tupp McComber blood, secured through the Tuttle cockerel.

The most perfect colored Rose Comb male ever produced was Mr. Bean's first prize Boston and New York cockerel (1910). He was valuable. Mr. Bean was offered $1,000.00 for this bird and four females. This is a bona fide offer, no valuation placed for advertising purposes, and there is no doubt but what he is the most valuable Rhode Island Red yet produced and the above short history of how the Bean strain originated will be of great value to intending beginners in Reds. One good male and one good female can start a strain. Have patience. It took Mr. Bean nine years to accomplish what some believe should be done in one or two seasons. Mr. Bean used a bird hatched from Tuttle's eggs that wasn't good enough to show, yet Mr. Bean saw something in him that he thought his strain needed. Brother Hewes is somewhat undecided as to the ability of the Red breeders to produce black tails. Mr. Bean produces many of them, but he will tell you that great as is his strain, yet he produces some culls, but they are culls only in the sense that they have too much color, too much black, and any of these so-called culls would produce show birds from a very mediocre lot of females. Perfection in a breading pen doesn't always insure a crop of high class show birds.

Dan Shove was one of the first to take up Reds. He also breeds Houdans, and good ones, but to compare the two breeds, as seen side by side, the comparison is very much in favor of the Reds. The big, long bodies of the Shove strain attracted my admiration. I didn't learn from Mr. Shove how and where he secured his strain, so I am unable to give facts concerning his birds.

Red Feather Farm, Fred Almy, proprietor, is a typical Rhode Island Red farm. It comprises 160 acres, but poultry is its staple. Mr. Almy makes a good living from his poultry and has saved money, besides. The Almy colony system works well and profitably with the Reds. He keeps them in flocks of 25 females presided over by 2 males, and 100 such flocks scattered systematically over the farm, present quite an attractive appearance. The Reds are fine, big, good shaped and of fair color. Mr. Almy, with the aid of one man, tends to his 1,500 old birds, besides raising 5,000 young ones. He uses a cart and horse to make his feeding rounds. Mr. Almy lately has taken to showing, and he had the goods requisite to win at New York and Boston. Mr. Almy's plant is well worth visiting. Much can be learned in the way of cheaply housing and caring for a monster flock of hens.

We found a very nice flock of Single Comb Reds upon the farm of C. A. Woodard, East Long Meadow, Mass. They were handsome, large, finely shaped and it would be difficult to beat them for looks as a flock. Mr. Woodard is quite a showman and it's quite hard to get the best of him. He says that they are a very profitable adjunct to the farm exchequer. He tried other breeds, but the Reds brought him in eggs and money during the cold winter months—something, he said, the others did not.

In the class with Lester Tompkins, Frank Read and President Bryant, as expert breeders of Single Comb Reds, we may safely rank A. C. Chapin, of Chicopee, Mass. Year after year he produces phenomenal birds. He has bred Reds for many years. Before taking up the Rose Combs, I. W. Bean bred Single Combs, and good ones. Mr. Chapin purchased a setting of eggs from him early one season. They hatched poorly, or Mr. Chapin had poor luck with the eggs. Later Mr. Bean replaced them with another setting. From this setting Mr. Chapin raised a cockerel that, mated with Mr. Chapin's own strain of females, founded a strain of Single Combs that is famous the country over. It's a strain that is noted for the extreme brilliancy of the color of the males. Many fine females are also produced and it's a strain that seems to nick with other strains. Mr. Chapin's matings always interested me. Mr. Chapin always looks for vigor in a bird in order to insure a good breeder, and he never breeds from a bird, either male or female, that has not an active, lively disposition. Dull, phlegmatic birds, according to his theory, never produce. Mr. Chapin is a State inspector of cattle and his duties outside of raising chickens is to inspect hogs on the slaughtering days at the Springfield refinery, thus attesting to the fact that Mr. Chapin is another poultryman that has scientific attainments. It is needless to state that Reds, as viewed on Mr. Chapin's place, are handsome to look at.

Up in Holyoke, Dick Lowcock, the good-natured policeman fancier, showed me a very pretty flock of Rose Combs. His strain is made up of the Prickett and Tuttle blood.

In Chatham, New York, one can view a very nice flock of Rose Comb Reds, the property of Messrs. Jenkins & Parke. They were about the first to take up the Reds in New York State, and they always raise good ones. A cockerel of their raising, mated with a hen we presented to them, produced females that have seldom been equaled, and the result of this union still plays a very important part in Messrs. Jenkins & Parke's flock. You can always see nice birds on their place, and in goodly numbers.

William Hazelton, of Hudson, New York, has a good looking flock of Reds, mostly Single Comb, and they have been a source of considerable profit to him, and the ad sometimes seen in papers, "Money in Reds," can be very well applied to Mr. Hazelton's case. We presented him with a cockerel that had his leg broken. He brought him home, nursed him, cured him and showed him, winning the blue for him. This bird was a full brother to the first prize and

champion male at New York, season of 1908-9, and he has been a valuable breeder for Mr. Hazelton.

Jordan Philip, treasurer of the city of Hudson, in conjunction with Mr. Harry Hermance, is breeding Single Comb Reds on quite an extensive scale. They paid big prices and purchased the best to start and they have met with good success. They had bred other varieties, but forsook them for Single Comb Reds, as they found them the best layers. As they cull very closely, one will only see fine specimens upon their breeding yards, hence their flock presents an attractive appearance.

One of the very first to take up the Reds was George W. Van De Veer, one of the leading agriculturists in the State of New York. Mr. Van De Veer is also a great scholar; orator, as well as a poet, and he is a credit to the ranks of the breeders of Reds. Mr. Van De Veer has the best blood attainable in all kinds of stock, and his blooded horses, cattle and swine always carry off the honors at the leading fairs. He tried the Reds alongside the other breeds and he found them the best by far. One can always see a nice flock on his handsome farm just outside of Amsterdam, New York. He is a kind, generous soul, and has helped many a beginner on the road to success, and it is always a great pleasure to call and spend a few hours talking chickens with him.

One of the prettiest flocks of Rose Comb Reds we ever witnessed was found on J. B. Burleigh's modest farm at Vernon, N. Y. If all flocks of Reds presented as handsome an appearance as does Mr. Burleigh's, there soon would be no other breeds. Mr. Burleigh is an old fancier, always being able to produce winners. He did with Barred Rocks and he does the same with Reds. He keeps his strain up to size by judicious mating, constantly improving their shape and color. This strain is a cross of Tuttle and Baerman blood. He secured one cockerel from eggs purchased from Mr. Tuttle some years ago that was a wonder, and this bird's blood exerted a great influence on his females. Vernon is cold in winter, but Reds thrive and lay, warm or cold.

Dr. Lee Smith, of Watertown, and Chester Hartley, of Gouverneur, New York, are among the breeders that I visited. They both have some nice birds. Mr. Hartley tried his Rose Comb Reds alongside his White Leghorns and the Reds outlaid the Leghorns.

Chester Long, of New Scotland, New York, has a nice looking flock of Rose Combs. He also tried them with White Leghorns and found the Rose Comb Reds the best layers, the Reds outlaying the Leghorns in winter.

James E. Van Alstyne, of Kinderhook, New York, has made a success of poultry and it's Reds that did it. He has a great utility strain, always laying, winter and summer, and he has produced a large number of high class birds. Six years ago we furnished him with a cockerel that, mated with his own hens, produced a wonderful flock of females. He afterwards sold a number of them to a noted dealer in Reds and they and some cockerels he sold him won for him at some very good shows. Mr. Van Alstyne is an intelligent breeder and his flock is valuable from a utility point of view and they look well as a flock, and clear Mr. Van Alstyne about $1,000 a year.

Peter Roap is a Kinderhook farmer that has a handsome flock of Reds. He secured his foundation blood from us. He secured a cockerel of fine Chapin blood. This Chapin cockerel was mated to a daughter of first New York, raised from eggs secured from us. Mr. Roap raised a number of pullets from this union that were of wonderful quality. Upon our return from Ellenwood Poultry Farm we secured these pullets and the old daughter of first New York, and from these pullets, seven winning females were produced last season that won at Madison Square, viz: 1st, 2d and 5th pullets, and four pullets that were in a winning pen besides a number of winners at other noted shows. Some may wonder how, after selling every bird I owned, I could start up so quickly again and produce winners for such shows as New York, Chicago and Baltimore. The above will explain it. We always mate up Mr. Roap's birds for him, so when I got stock I knew what I was getting. It isn't anything new for a strain to owe its existence to one bird, and I owe my present strain to the wonderful potency of the pullet that won first at New York, 1907-8, and I can show any visitor great-granddaughters of hers that look just about like her, only longer in body and better in eye. The pullet winning first at New York for the late lamented Mr. Gardner was a great-granddaughter of hers. Blood will tell. I am breeding from one pen that contains a daughter, three granddaughters and five great-granddaughters of the pullet first at New York, 1907-8. I was offered $75.00 for this pullet at that time. Mr. Jonas Hayner, the noted Barred Rock breeder, of Livingston,

N. Y., strongly advised me not to sell her, and I finally took his advice. Her memory is worth a good deal to me now. My present Rose Combs I secured from Mr. I. W. Bean, and I guess they are good enough for anybody.

On my way from the Chicago show, I stopped off for several hours and inspected Mr. Irving A. Sibley's Old Colony Strain Rose Comb Reds. I liked Mr. Sibley's exhibit at Chicago, one cockerel impressing me as about the best breeding cockerel I saw that season. In looking over Mr. Sibley's flock I couldn't help but admire its shape, and Rhode Island Red shape predominated, and I will mention right here that a flock of true shaped Reds cannot be surpassed in beauty by a flock of any other breed, even if they are not so good in color. Now, when I refer to not so good in color, I mean that they were faded in color; not yellow—the day of the yellow-Red female is gone. I didn't believe Mr. Sibley sent his best birds to Chicago, and I told him so and asked him how he came to leave certain females at home. "Well, to be frank with you, George, I had Mr.——— score my birds for me, and he picked out my exhibit. He sent the birds that scored the highest." We don't believe in the score-card and the fallacy of it was proven right in this instance. It was a pleasure to view Mr. Sibley's Reds, and it's quite a pleasure to meet Mr. Sibley. He is one of Indiana's leading business men and he has frequently been importuned to be a candidate for Congress in his district. He is a cousin of Congressman Sibley, of Pennsylvania, who has been elected both as a Republican and a Democrat.

Pennsylvania has many good breeders of Reds within her borders, including Craig & Mapes, Charles Shields, Charles Ober, E. S. Shelly, Edw. S. Lambrite, Annesly Anderson, Jake Sheibel, Mr. Robert F. Whitmer, owner of the Ellenwood Poultry Farms, also Winona Poultry Farms, at Lansdale, Pa. The only farms that we visited were Annesley Anderson's, Winona Farms and, of course, Ellenwood Poultry Farm. Annesly Anderson has fine looking birds, Rose Combs are his delight, and he has a noted strain. He purchased a cockerel from I. W. Bean last season, and he made a wonderful nick with his females. First pen at New York, was a product of this mating, also second pullet of Ellenwood Poultry Farm. I don't believe it will sound good for me to say very much about the Reds owned on that place, as it's a matter of history that I sold every bird I owned and moved them to Ellenwood. We showed them one season, winning at New York, among other prizes, champion male, and Mr. Lord, their present manager, made an enviable record the past season.

Winona Farms breed Reds mostly on account of their utility value and as they also breed S. C. White Leghorns, I had an opportunity to notice the difference in the looks of the two breeds, and the Reds didn't suffer by the comparison.

Mr. Wixon is a leading manufacturer of Lansdale, but he finds poultry raising both profitable and healthy.

The State of Maine has many Red breeders within its borders, notable among them being the general secretary of our club, George P. Coffin, his brother, Harry, who breeds very fine Rose Combs, capable of winning at Boston shows, also Mr. Morton, of Freeport, who breeds fine Single Combs. The breeders whose flocks I viewed are Thomas Primm, of Portland, and George Wiseman, of Lewiston. Mr. Primm raises Single Combs good enough to win at Boston, and he had some very nice birds upon his place. Mr. Wiseman has a 160-acre farm and he raises about 5,000 Single Comb Reds during a season. Mr. Wiseman visited the Boston show several years ago and gave the boys a taste of the Maine Reds. He got his own original stock from a Mr. Gunston, who I believe now resides in California. With him the Reds pay handsomely, and at the time of my visit, early in December, they were shelling out the eggs by the hundreds. He had about 1,500 layers and they were a very fine flock of poultry. One would have to travel many miles before he would see a handsomer lot. Mr. Wiseman once owned the celebrated "Johnny Wiseman," the fastest horse ever produced in the State of Maine. Outside of his poultry farm Mr. Wiseman owns quite a bunch of real estate.

W. F. Burleigh, Larrabee's Point, Vermont, had some good looking Rose Combs when we visited his place. He is situated just across the lake, opposite Fort Ticonderoga. Mr. Burleigh is making a great hustle for the Rose Comb Club, being a very efficient secretary.

We visited Newport, Rhode Island, with the intention of inspecting Philip Caswell's stock, but unfortunately, Mr. Caswell was away, so we only gave them a casual look through the fence. We saw some splendid looking birds, and riding by the handsome grounds, the looks of the fine Reds greatly added to the beauty of Mr. Caswell's place, but we didn't go out to his farms upon which his birds are raised.

We had quite a pleasant visit with Mr. Sherman and we found him very well posted on Red history.

A. G. Schirmer, of Princeton and H. E. Cole, of Trenton, are the only New Jersey breeders that we visited. Mr. Cole breeds Rose and Single Combs and has shipped Reds to England, and they pleased his purchasers. Mr. Cole informed us that the cause of the Reds is growing over in England, and it won't be very long before they will be generally bred over there, as they seem to surpass the English breeds in laying qualities. Mr. Schirmer breeds Reds mostly for pleasure; they appeal strongly to his fine artistic nature, and he firmly believes that they are the handsomest fowl on earth. We almost forgot that we visited Magnolia Poultry Yards, Magnolia, New Jersey, where we saw some very fine utility Reds. They were also of exhibition quality; Mr. Crossby, the owner, cleared over $600.00 last season besides attending to his business. He says it takes the Reds to do it.

Pine Croft Poultry Farm, Lenox, Mass., breeds Rose Combs good enough to win at New York. They raise about 2,000 each year, selling many for broilers and having a fancy egg trade, besides selling eggs for hatching and stock for exhibition purposes. The Rose Comb Reds here fill the bill exactly, and they certainly please the owner and would please the most fastidious for looks, and the quality of the meat upon their plump carcasses seem to please the many high-toned city people that live in and visit in Lenox. As broilers and roasters the Rhode Island Red is equaled by few and surpassed by no other breed.

In my trips through Connecticut the popularity of the Reds over other breeds was quite noticeable, in Hartford and vicinity, especially. Mr. Tuttle's fame as a breeder attracted the attention of his neighbors, as we may term them, to the breed. One man's success in any venture always attracts others to the possibilities of said venture. If Mr. Tuttle is successful, why not we? Or, if we secure some Tuttle stock, why cannot we do as well as he, hence the popularity of Reds in Connecticut can be attributed largely to Mr. Tuttle's connection with them. Another potent factor was the great popularity of Mr. E. L. Prickett, for some years secretary of the Rhode Island Red Club of America. He is a sincere, conscientious man and the earnest work done by him during his incumbency of the office he filled so acceptably did a wonderful lot of good for the Reds, and it was a matter of great regret that his business compelled him to refuse to accept the office any longer. We visited Mr. Prickett some years ago. We found him at his office in the powder mill, which was located at Hazardville. He showed me the ribbons and cups that adorned his office walls and desks, trophies won by his Rose Comb Reds, but they didn't interest me to the extent they would have if I had viewed them in other quarters. I never had much experience with powder, and I was very much relieved when Mr. Prickett said we will go to my place and look at my Reds. I learned a few things from Mr. Prickett: one of them was that an old gentleman by the name of Dennis bred some great Rose Comb Reds. This same Mr. Dennis states that many years ago the Red males were wonderfully rich red birds of rich undercolor, free from smut, tails of a glossy black and wings marked as we desire them today, and they come with both Rose and Single Combs; hence, we are forced to the inevitable conclusion that the Reds of 35, 40 and 50 years ago are the type of bird that we are fast getting back to. Thirty-five years ago a neighbor of ours had a cock bird that attacked a younger brother of mine. From the results of this attack, Willie (my brother's name) carried a scar until his death. This cock bird was a rich, brilliant red, of fine shape. His superior would be hard to find at the present day. Mr. S. Kinkle, the owner, called him a Red Shanghai. His legs were free from feathers and he was a Single Comb. There were Reds, and good Reds even in those days, so instead of being a new breed, they are really an old breed revived and named. Mr. Prickett was obliged to leave Hazardville, having been transferred to another plant, but he is back at the old stand again, and with Mr. Joseph McNamaro, another Rose Comb Red breeder of great prominence, to help boost, Hazardville, Connecticut, will once more be very prominent on the Red map.

Mr. Arthur Bailey, of Cobalt, the Payne Bros., of Portland; Mr. Townsend, of Danbury, and Wallace Pierson, of Cromwell, are breeders of Reds that we have visited. Mr. Bailey does nothing but raise chickens and deal in an occasional herd of cattle. He bred Single Comb Reds exclusively for a great many years and had good success with them, but several years ago, wishing new blood, he secured several males from A. C. Chapin, of Chicopee, Mass., and the union of Chapin blood with his own made a wonderful nick. He has a flock that is hard to beat, and during the last two years he has produced some of the best exhibition specimens. His flock looks very attractive and fetches him in a good income, winter and summer.

The Payne Brothers own a very large farm, and they breed Rose Comb Reds exclusively. They secured their start in exhibition stock from Mr. Tuttle and they raise good ones. They breed strictly for fancy, and don't have a very large flock, and every one kept is an exhibition bird, and it follows that they have a handsome appearing flock.

Mr. Townsend has only lately taken up the Reds, but he secured good ones. From them he bred a pullet and cockerel last season that were about as good as there were out. He started with utility stock, which was not of very good color, but he is an old breeder of other varieties and he knows how to breed from the good ones. He gave up the Rocks for Reds, and he is well satisfied, as he finds them far superior as layers.

Mr. Wallace Pierson, of Cromwell, has only bred Reds for two seasons, yet he is there with the goods and he got there this way: He secured eggs and several pullets and a cock from Lester Tompkins. He came to the New York show last year and purchased third prize Single Comb cockerel. He mated this cockerel with the best of his pullets, raised from Tompkins's eggs, and last season he could show you a handsome flock as a result of this mating—an example of how to start a winning strain at once. He breeds them for pleasure and he finds them handsome to look at and Mr. Pierson's way of starting could be very well followed.

Charles Thompson's Poultry Farm, at Lynnfield Center, Mass., is the home of several breeds, and here we could easily see the real beauty of a nice flock of Reds as compared with good Barred Rocks and White Wyandottes. Mr. Thompson has them both, but the Reds exceed them in beauty as a flock. He had very fine shaped birds, and of large size, and although his females had faded out, still they acquitted themselves, as far as looks were concerned, with the Barred Rocks and White Wyandottes, and the laying qualities of the Reds surpassed the other breeds on the place, and right here I will mention that where other breeds are kept along with Reds, the Reds invariably outlay the others.

Harvey Whitmyre, of Schenectady, N. Y., has some very good appearing Reds upon their yards. Mr. Whitmyre had a city plant, and his Single Comb Reds flourished in their modest quarters and they were handsome.

Mr. S. W. Melindy, of South Easton, Mass., had a nice flock of Single Combs and a few Rose Combs. They were nice appearing birds and some cracker-jacks were to be seen.

White Birch Poultry Farm has a winning line of Single Comb cockerels that would appeal to any lover of fine poultry, and their females have splendid type. At the time of my visit they were heavy in moult, so of course I couldn't see them at their best. Mr. I. W. Bean for many years bred Single Combs, but finding his place too small for both varieties, he sold his good ones to White Birch Poultry Farm. Dr. Conant, the owner, is a wealthy physician and surgeon of great repute in Boston, but he has an able manager and superintendent in William Withington, an old Red man. White Birch Farm is noted for winning first cockerel at both New York and Boston the same season.

In the course of my article I have mentioned only the flocks of those breeders that I personally inspected and I can truthfully state that for looks, the Reds are up with the most popular breeds. For utility value, I firmly believe that they excel all other varieties. They fill any want. They are fine looking show birds. The best Reds in a show room are generally the handsomest birds in the show room. They are easily reared; are uniformly healthy (any kind of an old house will do to shelter them in winter); they stand all climates; to the beginner they are the best breed to start with, as they are the easiest breed to select your show birds from; they are an easy breed to start in with, as a person learns to breed good Reds in a very short time, and there is room in the Red ranks. When you start in, get a few good birds and stick to them for several years. The progeny from the first mating may not satisfy you. Bunch your chicks so you can accurately mate up birds of the proper blood lines. Brother and sister are apt to produce nice color, but weak constitutions or white earlobes. By proper mating, what may apparently look like a bad mating may produce cracker jacks. It took nine years of patient effort on the part of I. W. Bean to place his Rose Combs where they are today. Lester Tompkins has been breeding them, or they were in his family, for thirty-five years, so don't be discouraged if you don't produce a satisfactory one in two or three

years. Don't be afraid to have confidence in your own strain, and don't be afraid to breed a bird that has a few imperfections, such as pepper on the wings of the females or purple or black on the wings of the male. Don't be alarmed if your males don't all come the same shade of red. There are a good many good shades of red and no one can tell you which is the proper shade. Suit yourself. The artists themselves disagree as to what constitutes good red color, so don't worry over the shade of red. Don't patronize any advertiser that says he has Reds in his pens that score 96 or 95. A Red that will score 90 is a good one. When you mate up your pens, don't leave out the important fact that congeniality is very much to be desired in a pen of breeders. Every female must have an affection for the male and vice versa. Don't forget the important part good rearing has on a Red. Give plenty to eat at all times. Don't find fault with an old line judge if he doesn't agree with you,—it doesn't show good taste. A whole lot of Red breeders don't agree with each other as to what constitutes a good Red, and in a vast majority of cases the best judging is done by the old line judge. A lot of fellows are criticising Theo. Hewes for suggesting methods of mating that will produce good Reds, claiming that as he never bred Reds his knowledge of mating them up for good results are consequently limited. We know from experience that Mr. Hewes knows something of what constitutes a good Red. At New York, Judge Riggs passed a cockerel of ours by without placing him. I asked Mr. Hewes why he thought he did it. I afterwards asked Mr. Riggs the same question and he gave me the very reason that Mr. Hewes had suggested. I know several good breeders that have their Reds mated up every season by Judge Cards, and I know know that they were mated for results, as they produced.

Judge Billy Russell mated up a noted Western exhibitor's pens every season, and they produced winners. If you can breed Reds for a year and have a good knowledge of them at the end of that time, why cannot an old line judge learn as quickly as yourself?

Kicking on decisions is not boosting a breed. Don't forget that the Standard for the Reds is settled for awhile. Eight hundred members of the Rhode Island Red Club of America voted to retain the present Standard, even if it was imperfect. They wanted it just as it was. They didn't delegate any member of the club to change it. They wanted it left just as it was; it was dear to their hearts; it brought from obscurity the greatest breed of fowls the world has ever known. No one can claim to have originated them. The nearest record we have of origination is the McComber strain, a hen from which established the Rose Comb Reds where they are today. Before Mr. Tuttle's strain appeared, there was but small hopes for the Rose Combs. President Bryant had secured some Pure McComber Rose Comb stock. He mated them up and bred from them. He sold a setting of eggs to Mr. Tuttle, from which he produced the Great St. Louis World's Fair, New York and Boston hen. This hen gave Mr. Tuttle's strain the great color. Breeders from all parts of the country secured eggs or stock from Mr. Tuttle and the Rose Comb Reds were saved. And later, when Mr. Tuttle's strain was, from constant inbreeding, losing its size, he again looked around for something to replenish his fast weakening strain. A new "Bryant," so far as Rose Combs are concerned, had appeared in the person of I. W. Bean, of South Braintree, Mass. Mr. Bean's stock was beginning to encroach upon Mr. Tuttle's in the show room. Their magnificent shape and size, as well as color appealed to him. He saw where he could again build, and he purchased some Bean females and they nicked with his males and Mr. Tuttle was again in a fair way to maintain his prestige as the greatest breeder of Reds that ever lived. It was very unfortunate for the Tuttle strain that Mr. Bean, after great effort, was able to secure one mediocre cockerel from Mr. Tuttle, through purchasing eggs. For some unexplained reason Mr. Tuttle would never price a high class bird to Mr. Bean. He sold him $8.00 birds, but with all this, the union of the Bryant-McComber blood with Mr. Bean's Park-Savage blood, blended to a remarkable degree and the famous Bean strain of Rose Combs was founded. I stumbled upon the clue that led to my questioning Mr. Tuttle as to how he originated his strain, and he told me the above facts. It will surprise many, but it is the truth. I guess the readers of this book have read enough of my ramblings, so I will conclude, with the wish that the Reds will continue to grow into favor and all Red breeders, from the North, East, South and West, will unite, and with one grand boost, shove so far in the van of all other breeders that American Poultrydom with one accord will acclaim America's Greatest Fowl to be—the Rhode Island Red.

Made in the USA
Las Vegas, NV
20 March 2025

19874981R00031